Advance praise for

Guide to Sea Kayaking
in Southern Florida

"From detailed site descriptions to practiced planning advice, Foster's latest work is a Southern Florida sea kayaker's classic. Throw this book in your cockpit and go!"
    —*Paddler* magazine

Help Us Keep This Guide Up to Date

Every effort has been made by the author and the editors to make this guide as accurate and useful as possible. However, many things can change after a guide is published—new products and information become available, regulations change, techniques evolve, etc.

We would love to hear from you concerning your experience with this guide and how you feel it could be improved and kept up to date. While we may not be able to respond to all comments and suggestions, we'll take them to heart and we'll also make certain to share them with the editors. Please send your comments and suggestions to the following address:

The Globe Pequot Press
Reader Response/Editorial Department
P.O. Box 833
Old Saybrook, CT 06475

Or you may e-mail us at: *editorial@globe-pequot.com*

Thanks for your input, and happy travels!

Regional Sea Kayaking Series

Guide to Sea Kayaking in Southern Florida

The Best Day Trips and Tours from St. Petersburg to the Florida Keys

by

Nigel Foster

The Globe Pequot Press

Old Saybrook, Connecticut

Cover design: Adam Schwartzman
Text design: Casey Shain
Cover photograph: Mary Ann Duffus
Maps by: Maryann Dubé and Mary Ballacino

Photo Credits: Page 8: © Robert Starling Photography; pages 112, 117, 192: photos by Michael Gray; page 187: photo by Jamie Jackson. Photos on pages 4, 16, 25, 29, 35, 39, 45, 48, 51, 56, 61, 63, 74, 78, 86, 97, 103, 107, 125, 128, 140, 155, 159, 162, 170, 195, 200, 206, 213 and 225 are by Nigel Foster.

Library of Congress Cataloging-in-Publication Data
Foster, Nigel.
    Guide to sea kayaking in southern Florida: the best day trips and
    tours from St. Petersburg to the Florida keys / by Nigel Foster. —1st
ed.
        p.   cm. (Regional sea kayaking series)
    Includes bibliographical references (p.) and index.
    ISBN 0-7627-0336-9
    1. Sea kayaking—Florida—Guidebooks.   2. Natural history—
Florida—Guidebooks.   3. Florida—Guidebooks   1. Title.
GV776.F6F67   1999
917.59—dc21   99-12395
                                                          CIP

Manufactured in the United States of America
First Edition/First Printing

To Larry Willis, who first introduced me to the delights of Florida paddling.

The Loxahatchee River owes its pristine appearance in large part to the untiring efforts of Larry, a native Floridian. By his example he motivated groups of local paddlers to haul out mountains of "junk" from the river and its banks. He even created the exclusive "Bottom Feeders" club of those paddlers who could retrieve discarded cans from the bottom while performing a kayak roll. Years of effort on his part has noticeably improved the quality of a trip down the river.

For your active part in improving the quality of a Florida paddling environment, I dedicate this book to you. May your example be an inspiration to us all.

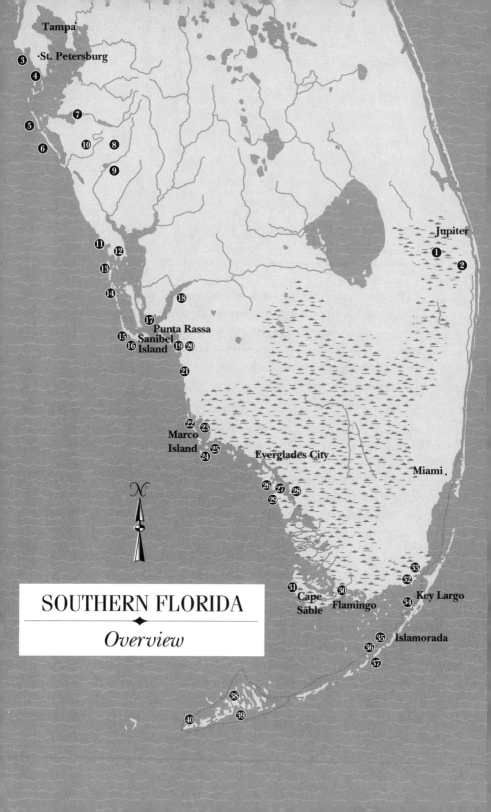

SOUTHERN FLORIDA
Overview

Tampa

·St. Petersburg

Jupiter

Punta Rassa
Sanibel
Island

Marco
Island

Everglades City

Miami .

Cape
Sable

Flamingo

Key Largo

Islamorada

N

Contents

Appendices

Acknowledgments

People can be so great! I was constantly refreshed by the degree of help offered throughout the preparation of this guide, and I am grateful for so many contributions which have enriched the book and my own experience. To all those named below and all those who helped but are not named individually, thank you!

Mr. Adams in the Boothe Bird museum unlocked his stuffed heron. Chris Siegfried contributed several excellent routes and tirelessly replied to my queries. Joy Williams unwittingly supplied me with an idyllic writing environment, complete with "Chuck-will's-widows," in Florida, through the hospitality of my friends, Tom Pogson and Laura Pomeroy. Bill and Ellen Palmer in Key West shared some wonderful trips. Scott Williams lent me a kayak, joined me on several excellent routes, and on sultry evenings on remote beaches produced from his kayak the most wonderful red wines! Contributing photographer, Robert Starling, added the caviar, exotic cheeses, crackers, and vintage port.

The owner of By the Bay Outfitters described local trips and turtle watches and replaced my plastic Ziploc with a waterproof case for my GPS. (It remains leakproof!) Michael Gray contributed paddling anecdotes and photographs. Peter and Elizabeth Foster helped with research. Larry Willis, Nancy Paysen, the staff of Florida Bay Outfitters, Eric Bailey, and Jim Traverse all contributed information that enrich the text. Mary Anne Duffus offered the front cover photograph.

Kristin Nelson showed me it's possible to check the ads in the morning paper for cheap used cars, and by evening be mobile in the Coup-de-Ville Cadillac from which I explored Florida. She also fearlessly posed in front of alligators, sought information for me with relentless determination, and encouraged me throughout the preparation of this book. I exaggerate only her fearlessness.

Finally, thanks to Laura Strom, Christina Lester, and all of the hardworking Globe Pequot team.

Map Legend

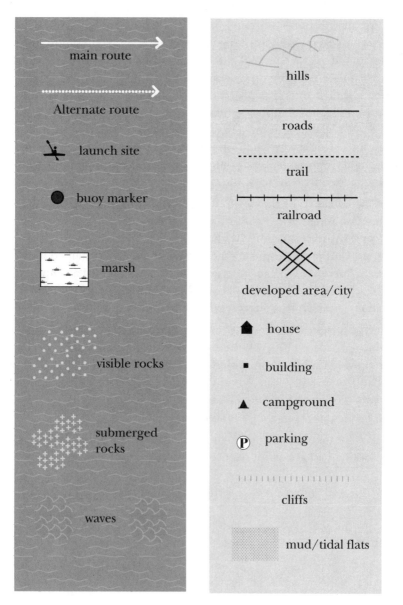

WATER

main route

Alternate route

launch site

buoy marker

marsh

visible rocks

submerged rocks

waves

LAND

hills

roads

trail

railroad

developed area/city

house

building

campground

parking

cliffs

mud/tidal flats

Introduction

Snow on the tracks was causing delays and cancellations. I'd gotten halfway to the airport and I had expected the warmth of a train carriage along the Welsh coast instead of this drafty railway platform. I stamped my feet on the cold concrete and watched thin snakes of snow blow past to build up against my baggage. "Ha! We could be snowed in for a few days here if this continues," a fellow would-be passenger commented in a far too gleeful tone. "Great! A few days off work. Why should I mind?"

I didn't share his sentiments. I was trying to escape to Florida. Although it looked as though I'd been thwarted, I turned out to be lucky in the end. A train finally got through and it reached the airport in time for me to catch my flight. So I skipped from airport to airport until, shortly after dark, I was reunited with my bags at the baggage carousel in Florida. When I stepped though the glass doors into the moist heat of West Palm Beach airport, I grinned in pleasure. It was warmer outside in the night air than in the temperature-controlled terminal. Flowers scented the air with a sweetness that reminded me a little of evening primrose, and a little of the humid scents in the hothouses of the Kew Botanical Gardens in London. Silhouettes of palms stood like construction pillars beyond the road.

Southern Florida—a perfect winter paddling destination, where it's possible to rent a kayak almost wherever you choose to go, and where a wilderness experience is around every corner. A place where if paddlers tell you they see dolphins almost every day, they actually mean about seven days a week. A place where the tangle of mangrove islands around the coast makes exploration stimulating, yet also creates shallow water with plenty of sheltered paddling with a lot to see. Once you're out among the mangroves, you usually share the experience only with the wildlife and your companions. Paddle, swim, snorkel, sunbathe, or watch the birds; the climate is just right for doing it all in comfort, and there are trips to suit every mood.

I've detailed some useful general information, tips, and cautions in this introduction. Throughout the book you'll find sidebars offering insights into other facets of Florida. Browse the guide and, for example, you'll find crocodile information lurking close to the description of routes where you might be lucky enough to see one of these creatures.

You'll find information about Calusa Indians tucked alongside the description of routes where you can see their ancient shell mounds. I've also included information about some of the wildlife centers, interpretive centers, and museums that might help you learn more about the area and thus enrich your paddling experience.

Among the forty trips profiled in this guide are some for the committed paddler and some for the beginner. You'll also learn about places where you can enroll in guided tours with people who know the area, if you want the personal approach, and about a few places where you can take lessons in warm water to master skills. However you choose to paddle, I wish you lots of fun.

Kayaks and Equipment

Paddlers in Florida have a different approach to the sport than sea kayakers in many other parts of the United States. I see people out enjoying paddling trips in fully equipped, standard sea kayaks, but enormous numbers of paddlers make similar trips aboard sit-on-top (undecked) kayaks, in general touring kayaks, in white-water kayaks, on surf-racing skis (narrow, tippy, and fast sit-on-top sprint-racing kayaks, often used in warm locations for flat-water touring), and in open canoes. Many people travel in double kayaks as well as singles. There appears to be far more emphasis on what you are doing and where you are going than on how you are doing it. If you've been a "purist" sea kayaker so far, this could be a good opportunity to try other types of kayaks and assess their suitability to this unique environment.

In renting a kayak in Southern Florida, you may find your choice limited to sit-on-tops. Rental companies may allow car-topping or offer a drop-off service, but not always; some permit paddling only from their own beach. Rental cars generally don't have roof racks, and the correct rack may be difficult to locate and expensive to obtain. If you plan to rent a car, bring along mini-cell cushioning pads with load-securing straps, and plenty of rope, to hold your kayaks to the roof.

I like to carry my own take-apart paddle with me when I travel to Florida, as the choice offered with rentals doesn't always excite me. However, the shallow waters and the occasional impact with oyster beds cause more wear than all my rough-water paddling elsewhere. You may want to use your second-best paddle instead of your best.

I always wear a personal flotation device (PFD)—a life jacket. If you don't wear your PFD all the time, secure it so it is readily accessible. Out on the water, you can receive an on-the-spot fine if you cannot show that you have a PFD on board.

Tips for Paddling in Southern Florida

Even if conditions seem set for the perfect holiday, there are still a few quirks of Florida's character you should know about, and some safety tips worth bearing in mind. For example, hot humid weather can cause thunderstorms. Hurricanes, tornadoes, and severe storms don't roll in on a daily basis, but they do occasionally make some changes in the landscape. And the sun gets hot enough to damage skin.

Keep the following tips in mind as you set off on a kayaking trip in this region.

Know Your Limits

Only you know your paddling ability in different conditions. Many trips in this guide keep to sheltered water with a short *fetch* (distance the wind can blow uninterrupted across the water), where waves will be small. If in doubt about your ability to cope with challenging conditions, take one of these sheltered trips. On more exposed trips beware of offshore winds, as these produce rougher conditions the farther from land you're blown. Rough water will also result when the wind blows against the current. Although you can explore much of the Southern Florida coast with very low risk, it's essential you assess the suitability of each trip, your paddling ability, and the expected conditions before you set out, and if in doubt choose something safer.

Get a Weather Forecast

Weather reports on weather stations, radio, and television will give you warning of winds, thunder, heat, and humidity. You'll often also pick up the static crackle of thunder some distance away on a radio, which provides another warning if you happen to be listening. Thunderstorms are usually associated with strong winds, so beware of local winds as well as lightning.

Southern Florida has two seasons: summer and winter. Winter is the best paddling season, but if you visit Florida in the heat and humidity of summer, then the most pleasant place to be is often out on the water.

In winter, from October through March, expect warm, dry, sunny weather. The night temperature on rare occasions drops as low as freezing, but the water remains warm. You'll need to be prepared for cold, but also for hot sun.

In summer, from April through September, expect hot, humid weather with regular thunderstorms, mostly in the afternoon and evening, and more bugs. At this time of year, start really early, as the heat arrives with the first glimpse of sun. Plan to be off the water by midday or early afternoon, before the thunderstorms arrive.

Hurricane season is in late summer, but hurricanes are few, and a lot of advance warnings are given. Tornadoes and waterspouts are possible at almost any time in hot, humid weather. Watch for storm clouds that look bubbly, like egg boxes underneath, and leave the water for shelter if you see such clouds approaching.

Storm clouds develop rapidly in Florida.

Use Sun Protection

Remember that you can still get sunburned on overcast days. The glare off the water increases your exposure to the sun, so you may find yourself frying. Take sunscreen, sun hat, and some clothes with long sleeves and full leg covering. Sunglasses are essential. I use polarized lenses, which cut the reflected light and enable me to see into the water better. There is so much sea life to observe that I really recommend the polarized glasses.

Use a Compass

Sea kayaking in Southern Florida is a sea-level sport in an area where most of the land is at about sea level also. Route finding and navigation can present an interesting challenge. Mangrove islands, which play a major role in the creation of the coastal landscape, can look identical to one another and are certainly not all marked on the charts. These islands don't stay the same; they grow and change shape as the mangroves spread, beginning again after each hurricane. New islands grow, yet the mangroves on the long-established islands may not be any different in height or appearance than on the more recent ones, making positive identification tricky. Only a few of the islands are named.

Use a compass to confirm your general direction and help you keep to the intended route. Be aware of the position of the sun in the sky in relation to your direction of travel so you'll notice if it suddenly appears somewhere else. For short periods, you can use the wind direction in a similar way. Practice aligning your chart with the landscape and with the compass so that you can more easily identify features around you.

Compass. I consider a compass indispensable in Southern Florida for helping me confirm my position or direction. It's easy to get turned around in the mangroves in cloudy weather. Use an orienteering type of fluid-filled compass. (If it's air-filled it will take in saltwater and become useless.) Attach your compass with a line to your kayak or clothing so you won't lose it should you drop it.

Note that true north is constant whereas the position of the magnetic north pole varies. All bearings in this book refer to true north and will need to be adjusted for use with a compass.

SAFETY TIPS FOR LIGHTNING

Always get a weather forecast. If storms are forecast, stay close to land and watch for the buildup of thunder clouds. Stormy days are not for open crossings. Look into the wind for approaching changes.

Always wear your personal flotation device (PFD) on the water. Carrying one is not sufficient. Many people survive lightning strikes, but if your body sinks, the chances of anyone retrieving and resuscitating you are slim.

Get off the water when a storm approaches. On open water you will be the most prominent point for a lightning strike. If you are close to taller objects, such as boats, you are in danger from electrical currents running through the water. There isn't anything you can do on the water to avoid the effects of lightning strike, so be prepared to get off the water quickly. At the earliest signs of a storm, seek a good spot on shore to shelter.

Seek well-drained broken ground if possible, and avoid drainage routes. The current from a strike will then run through the surrounding ground, following paths of low resistance, such as drainage routes.

Adopt a protective crouch position. Sit or crouch, on an insulating pad if possible, with hands on your lap. Keep all contacts with the ground as close together as possible. Your aim is to minimize ground contact so that an electric current will find no advantage in passing through you or, if it does, so that it passes through non-vital parts.

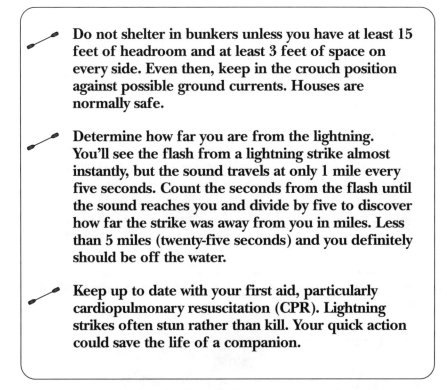

Do not shelter in bunkers unless you have at least 15 feet of headroom and at least 3 feet of space on every side. Even then, keep in the crouch position against possible ground currents. Houses are normally safe.

Determine how far you are from the lightning. You'll see the flash from a lightning strike almost instantly, but the sound travels at only 1 mile every five seconds. Count the seconds from the flash until the sound reaches you and divide by five to discover how far the strike was away from you in miles. Less than 5 miles (twenty-five seconds) and you definitely should be off the water.

Keep up to date with your first aid, particularly cardiopulmonary resuscitation (CPR). Lightning strikes often stun rather than kill. Your quick action could save the life of a companion.

GPS. I attempted to use a Global Positioning System (GPS) device in Florida, but found that the intricate mangrove passages made tracing routes too complicated. I reverted to the compass and to visual route finding, which in most cases here is much simpler. If you take a GPS, use special care to keep it dry. A little salt in these conditions of heat and high humidity wreaks havoc with sensitive instruments.

Pack Wisely

It's a good idea to take along a few of your own basic emergency supplies, even if you're renting a kayak. Pack such items as a simple first aid kit, repair tape, line for a makeshift towline if necessary, and bug repellent. If you're in an exposed or remote area, distress flares, cell phone, or emergency radio will give you a chance to attract help. Seal everything that's not waterproof inside waterproof containers. Take fresh water to avoid dehydration, and pack some extra food, just in case.

Land Safely

Landing is often difficult because of the awkward nature of mangroves, and sometimes because of private ownership or because the land is part of a historical or wildlife reserve. But the coastal water around much of Southern Florida is so shallow that it's possible to step out of your kayak into knee-deep water to stretch your legs.

In the Everglades, landing on the camping chickees, which are positioned where there's no dry land and consist of elevated platforms with roofs and toilets, can be tricky. Raft side-by-side with a companion so that your kayak is held steady while you clamber out and up. Unloading and reloading the kayaks at a chickee may be an even trickier procedure, requiring some balance. You'll probably do best to sit in another kayak while you unload your own, passing each item up to the platform above. Tether your kayaks on the downwind side so they do not scrape against the stanchions, or paddle a line to nearby mangroves and create a running mooring with which to later pull your kayaks out onto open water.

Camp Clean

The camping trips in this book make use of designated camping spots. In some places, you can camp wild, but these can be fragile environments. If you do camp, wild or otherwise, please minimize your impact on the environment and carry out all you took in. The sea life in these shallow waters is rich, and great to see, but it will not survive abuse.

Camping on chickees can be an interesting experience. Your tent must be freestanding because the wooden platforms will not take tent pegs, and nails are not permitted. Take line with you to thread between the boards to secure your tent. Gravity may not be sufficient if the wind blows, because gaps in the boards allow the wind to get underneath the tent.

Introduction

Cooking can be precarious on chickees because cutlery, plates, mugs, and food can easily blow off the edge or drop between the cracks into the water. Take a tarp or sheet to provide a crack-free floor. If your stove gets hot underneath, bring something to sit it on or you'll probably set fire to the wooden floor before your meal is cooked.

How to Use This Guide

Refer to the overview map on page vi to see the location in Florida of the trips included in this guide. The trips are discussed in the guide in geographical order, starting in the north and working south to the Florida Keys.

Each trip description includes travel directions to the launch site from main highways. Basic route maps mark the most significant features described in the text, although they are not intended as a substitute for the nautical charts indicated for actual navigation.

When selecting a route check the trip highlights as well as the trip rating, which gives an idea of the level of difficulty and provides cautions. If the trip looks suitable, read through the leading description to find out more about the trip and points of interest.

The directions for the trip consist of brief descriptions of various legs of the journey with some indications of mileages and landmarks, and points of interest on the way. This is the description that will guide you while on your trip; you should follow it through on the map step-by-step in preparation for your journey. You may find it useful to mark your chart with a waterproof pen to help you remember your route, and to take your guidebook with you in a waterproof bag.

Extra tips are sometimes given under the heading "Trip planning," and some suggestions for places to eat and places to stay are added at the end of the directions for the trip to give you further options if you wish to stay in the area.

Mileage

The mileages given in the text are in nautical miles, not in the statute miles used for distances on land. One nautical mile equates to one minute of latitude, or one sixtieth of a degree of latitude, and is the scale normally used for measuring distances on the sea. For comparison, a nautical mile equals about 1.15 statute miles, or about 1.85 kilometers. A knot is a measurement of speed that equals 1 nautical mile per hour. A tidal current moving at 4 knots is traveling at a speed of 4 nautical miles per hour.

Trip Rating and Duration

I rate each trip as Basic, Intermediate, or Advanced, according to its difficulty, but of course that's subjective. What one paddler considers easy is another paddlers' challenge, and weather conditions can alter a trip completely. Also, while the Basic trips were designed to be easier, they may certainly be enjoyed by more experienced paddlers. I also suggest the duration for a trip, say four hours for a short trip. My timings are rough guidelines for paddlers of approximately the level indicated in the trip rating. If you know your approximate normal paddling speed, you should be able to calculate a more accurate time for your own trips. It's often possible to complete a trip in a much shorter time than suggested—but it can be more rewarding to take your time.

Navigation Aids

Appropriate sea charts are listed for each trip. For some of the inland waterways, a topographical land map is your only choice, but will show everything you need. Nautical charts may be ordered from your local chart agent in advance, or picked up in Florida from marine stores.

The National Oceanic and Atmospheric Administration (NOAA) issues a free catalog, No. 1, to cover the charts of the Atlantic and Gulf coasts. The catalog also lists agents in the United States and abroad where you can order or buy charts. The catalog, and the charts themselves, can be ordered direct from Distribution Division (N/ACC 3), National Ocean Service, Riverdale, MD 20737–1199. Telephone orders are accepted, using Visa or MasterCard, at (301) 436–6990 or (800) 638–8972.

The waterproof charts detailed in this guide are produced by Waterproof Charts, 320 Cross Street, Punta Gorda, FL 33950, (www.waterproofcharts.com). Waterproof Charts produces a regional catalog of its charts. If you can't find the catalog or the charts locally, you can order direct by calling (800) 423–9026 or, from outside the United States, (941) 639–7626, fax (941) 637–9866. The e-mail address is sales@waterproofcharts.com. Where there's a choice, I find the large-print waterproof charts particularly useful.

Topographical maps made by the U.S. Geological Survey with a scale of 1:24,000 are detailed in this book only if there is no nautical chart available. Maps may be ordered from the U.S. Geological Survey, Denver, Colorado 80225, or Reston, Virginia 22092. They are identified by scale and by a name rather than a number.

Tidal Information

Tides in this region have a small range (generally less than 5 feet). Rising tides flow inland through channels between islands and bars, while falling tides flow outward to the outermost barrier islands. The tidal streams can be fast when a large body of water is channeled through a narrow gap, but most streams are weak. Local currents can be set up by the wind, affecting predicted tide times and the height of tides, so detailed planning can be somewhat inaccurate. A general awareness of the time of high water is usually sufficient to plan the day.

For some trips I recommend a start at a particular state of tide. Tide tables can be obtained from most marina stores in Southern Florida—and there are plenty of marinas. However, you'll probably do fine simply by asking someone for the time of high water, as trips in this region rarely require complex tidal calculations.

The Gulf Stream current runs northward along the Atlantic coast at a speed of 4 knots or more, but it is an offshore current, so not of concern for the trips in this guide.

In the collection of islands known as the Florida Keys, the tides are somewhat erratic. There are generally two tides per day on the Atlantic side of the Keys and only one per day on the Gulf of Mexico. An almost continuous flow moves from the Gulf to the Atlantic via the main channels, but the rate of flow varies with the state of the tide.

A good seat-of-the-pants approach to tidal planning is to make your trip around high tide so you can count on sufficient depth of water to paddle the route. If you find yourself paddling against the stream, follow the inside of each bend because the greatest flow is normally around the outside. Also, use eddies wherever possible. Eddies occur where the flow is obstructed, and take the form of slack water or water moving gently in the opposite direction to the main stream. Look on the downstream side of bridge stanchions, for example.

Directions for the Trip

This guide includes a sketch map for each trip. The travel directions given for every outing also can usually be followed using a standard road map. The DeLorme mapping company produces a road atlas and gazetteer, available from bookstores, or at (207) 846–7000 or www.delorme.com.

A word about parking: When I launched from the beach in Key West, I left my car parked on the road beside the beach, where there was free parking. When I returned, a road crew was busy planting poles that looked suspiciously like the ones that carry parking meters. Parking and launching information changes, so I'd really appreciate any feedback you can offer on changes that occur so that I can keep this guide up to date.

Natural History

Southern Florida wildlife is a significant feature of any paddling trip. The more you know, the more you see—and the more interesting it becomes. When I first visited Florida, I was bewildered. I was familiar with many northern European species of seabirds, plants, and trees. Some of the Florida species seemed similar, but many I'd never seen before. An identification book, such as Peterson's *Field Guide to the Birds of Eastern Land and Water*, can help a lot. Carry it in a waterproof bag on your trips and refer to it when you see species you don't recognize.

Some bird species are worth looking up before you go so you'll recognize them. I'd include the frigate bird, anhinga, white pelican, wood stork, roseate spoonbill, and limpkin. A trip to a refuge such as Pelican Man on Lido Key is a great help, because you can look closely at individual birds and check them against the identification boards at the refuge.

When it comes to birds of prey, there are many. You'll see ospreys, which nest on top of poles and pylons, making large piles of big sticks as nests. Ospreys are so common that the parrot at Southern Exposure Sea Kayaks in Tequesta can perfectly reproduce an osprey cry as part of its repertoire, mimicking the pair that frequents the parking lot. In some places you'll see huge osprey nests atop houseboats. Turkey vultures and black vultures also are common, circling in their dozens around thermal air currents, and bald eagles are found here too.

Marine animals in Florida can sometimes appear tame, although they are wild. Dolphins often swim quite close to investigate you with a curiosity that might match your interest in them. Manatees, which swim more slowly, may also check you out. Manatees have no dorsal fin, so when you see a broad, tan-colored back just at the surface you're probably looking at a manatee. Neither dolphins nor manatees are likely to overturn your kayak unless you run over them, so if you see them, relax and enjoy the experience.

On both fresh and brackish water, alligators are common. Keep your distance. Alligators seldom approach unless they have become accustomed to people, in which case they can become dangerous. Keep your distance, too, from young alligators, as there's usually a mother alligator around to protect her young. Swimming in places where there are alligators is foolish. Be aware that dogs are a favorite alligator food.

Crocodiles generally keep their distance. Crocodiles are mostly limited in range to an area of Florida Bay at the southern tip of the state, in salt water.

You'll see sharks and stingrays, barracuda and Portuguese man-of-war, and many other interesting creatures of the sea. Mostly they won't bother you. If you feel a bit nervous, just think how many people swim, snorkel, and dive in Florida every day without being attacked. However, avoid wading in murky waters, where shark attacks are more likely.

When you go wading, be watchful of jellyfish. Wear shoes of some sort to protect you from oyster shells and stingrays. Stingrays introduce venom into the wound they make with their tail. You need to get medical attention for such an injury, but you can help by applying heat to the affected area or immersing it in hot water. Monitor for signs of allergic reaction.

On and around shore, especially when camping, you may find snakes, scorpions, or biting spiders, but you're more likely to be troubled by fire ants. Watch for the sandy craters of their hills, and for tiny ants. The ant bite hurts and will generally form a pustule that may last for weeks. Flying insects abound, and a lot of them bite, too. Bring repellent, especially in summer when the bugs are most numerous. When camping, check your shoes before you put them on for creatures that might choose them for shelter. Likewise, take a cockpit cover for your kayak to keep out the bugs at night. I once endured a horde of earwigs aboard my kayak as I paddled across the English Channel to

France, but I'd be less happy to share my space with a brown recluse spider, or a scorpion!

Snakes are quite common in Southern Florida, but you're not likely to see any. Of about twenty-six species, four are venomous: the diamondback and pygmy rattlesnakes, the coral snake, and the cottonmouth. If you see a snake and you're at all uncertain about what it is, give it a wide berth. If you're unlucky enough to be bitten, the emergency number for the U.S. Poison Control Center in Tampa, Florida, is (813) 253–4444 or (800) 282–3171.

Florida is a rich paddling area. Once you become familiar with it you'll discover there are many good alternative trips and variations on your favorites. I hope you'll find this guide a useful introduction to new areas. May you too treasure paddling in southern Florida sufficiently to assist in sustaining and improving on the quality of this unusual paddling environment.

Introduction

Route 1:

━━ ━━ ━━ ━━ ━━ ━━ ━━ ━━ ━━ ━━ ━━ ━━ ━━ ⟶

The Loxahatchee River

The Loxahatchee River is one of my favorite Florida paddling trips. It is also the only designated National Wild and Scenic River in Florida. It is a popular canoe and kayak descent that retains a magical beauty and pristine quality surprisingly unaffected by the large numbers of visitors that pour down the river daily. This is to a great extent due to the cleanup efforts of the Coconut Kayakers Club under the energetic direction of local Southern Exposure Sea Kayaks shop owner Larry Willis and to the work of Eric Bailey of Canoe Outfitters of Florida.

The route follows the winding river from its upper reaches beneath a canopy of spectacular swamp cypress trees with a mix of tropical and temperate vegetation to emerge into a more open vista of mangroves and palms where the tannin-rich stream turns brackish at the tidal limit.

TRIP HIGHLIGHTS: The upper part of the river, with its whiskey-colored water and majestic swamp cypress trees, and turtles sunbathing on fallen logs. There's a chance you'll see alligators, and I've seen otters, too. Early in the day you may see deer along the swampy bank.

TRIP RATING:

Intermediate: The current in the top section strains through cypress knees and over two small man-made dams, requiring a degree of confidence and competence. Fallen trees sometimes block the river, and you'll need to pull around or over them, although blockages are soon removed by volunteers.

TRIP DURATION: For a full downstream trip to the Jonathan Dickinson State Park landing, allow about 5 or 6 hours, including breaks. Begin early in the day and take your time. With the twisting nature of this river, a full descent to the landing can be from 5 miles to 7.5 miles depending on how you measure it. A round-trip to Masden Dam from the launch site is 1.5 miles; allow about 2 hours.

NAVIGATION AIDS: Take the USGS topographic maps of the area, 1:24,000 scale, "Rood" and "Jupiter"; however, as you can only go two ways on the river—upstream and downstream—you'll get where you want to by following it, and will know where you are by noting the features.

TIDAL INFORMATION: The upper section of the river is freshwater, with no tides, and in the lower reaches the tidal flow is weak. If you intend to paddle the river to the sea, a good plan is to hit tidal water about an hour after the time of high water at Jupiter Inlet.

CAUTIONS: The dams can present a hazard, so get out to inspect and, if in doubt, portage. There are alligators on the river, and regulations stipulate no swimming.

TRIP PLANNING: Plan to leave early. Although the first part of the river is in shade and therefore deceptively cool, when you reach brackish water the shade disappears and the sun can be relentless. Don't forget to take sun precautions—take a hat, sunscreen, water, and a shirt. You will likely reach the last, unshaded section of the river at the hottest time of day, so be prepared!

LAUNCH SITE: Access the river from Jupiter Road, State Route 706, 1.3 miles west of Florida Turnpike exit 116 and 1–95 exit 59B. The launching bank is on the north side of the road, although plans call for it eventually to be on the south side. It is open from 8:00 A.M. till sundown. The concession building, where kayaks may be rented and a pickup from the end of the river may be arranged, lies down a short track to the south of the road, just before the river. Look for the sign that says Canoe Outfitters.

The Loxahatchee River

Launch into the stream, which will almost immediately carry you into a dense subtropical forest. Look for night herons and heavily scented swamp lilies (big, spidery, and brilliant white). Your first way-mark will be Lainhart Dam, just **a quarter mile** downstream.

Depending on the water level and your craft, you may wish to shoot this dam. But I would not recommend it at low water level except in a polyethylene kayak. You can get out before the dam at the canoe ramp and portage walkway on the left. Unfortunately the ramp is poorly suited for kayaks, leaving an awkward egress at most water levels, and the current contributes to the awkwardness of landing here.

Alligators often are found a few yards downstream from the dam.

From Lainhart Dam, the river weaves between tall swamp cypress with rich lower-level vegetation.

CAUTION: The banks are encumbered with knobby cypress "knees." Take care to avoid being pushed onto these spikes by the current; aiming toward the inside of each bend will help.

The next obvious way-mark is Masden Dam, **half a mile** past Lainhart Dam. If you're making the round-trip from the launch site to Masden and back, stand and watch the fun at the dam for a while, then begin your upstream leg.

Masden Dam maintains a certain water level in the swamp even in dry weather. Although it's frequently OK to shoot this dam in a kayak, you may wish to use the canoe portage boardwalk. If you decide to run the fall, the channel to the right is the better route.

CAUTION: The current runs swiftly into cypress knees and roots on the far bank immediately downstream of the fall, so take evasive action. We've found a radio, a camera, a wallet, many pairs of sunglasses, a hog's skull, fishing pole, and even beers on occasion in this tangle of roots. Don't contribute to the collection!

Downstream, the river continues to twist and turn for **half a mile** to the bridges of the Florida Turnpike and I–95. Here, rows of concrete supports create a bewildering pattern of reflections in a more open stretch of water that will give you the opportunity to relax for a moment.

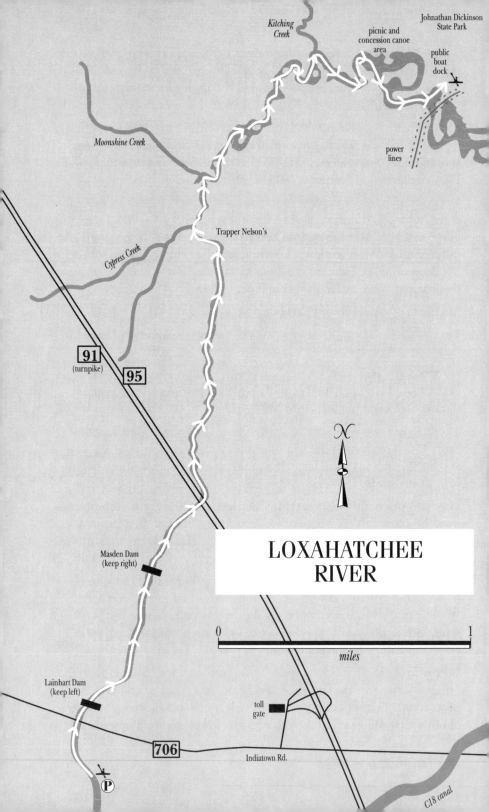

Kitching
Creek

picnic and
concession canoe
area

Johnathan Dickinson
State Park

public
boat
dock

Moonshine Creek

power
lines

Trapper Nelson's

Cypress Creek

91
(turnpike)

95

N

Masden Dam
(keep right)

LOXAHATCHEE
RIVER

0   1

miles

Lainhart Dam
(keep left)

toll
gate

706

Indiatown Rd.

P

C.18 canal

Now follows about **2 miles** of freshwater before you emerge into a pool bordered on the right by boat docks roofed in corrugated iron. This is Trapper Nelson's, the restored camp of the famed outdoorsman who died in 1968. It is worth taking a break here. Land on the boat dock and pull your kayak clear of the wooden walkway to leave the access free.

Trapper Nelson's lies at the downstream limit of the freshwater Loxahatchee. From here the vegetation changes to salt-tolerant species, notably mangrove and palm. You will lose the shelter of an overhead canopy as the river widens, and you may see manatees in addition to alligators.

The Jonathan Dickinson State Park main dock lies on the left bank, **2.5 miles** from Trapper Nelson's. Look for buildings on the bank and lines of rental canoes. There's a small dock and beach upstream of the main dock; use this instead of the rental boat launching area. Here are restrooms, a shop offering some refreshments, and information boards with details on local wildlife and history.

If you've arranged to be picked up by the canoe outfitters, paddle a short distance farther downstream to the park's public boat dock, which you'll find at the end of a small bay to the left of the river.

ADDITIONAL PADDLING: If you're looking for more travels, you can continue downstream for **4.5 miles** from the public dock toward Jupiter Inlet. You'll reach a twin set of bridges, one carrying a railroad, the other carrying Route 811. Pass beneath both bridges and take the next right branch to follow the Intracoastal Waterway south. Take the first left (east) channel by green channel marker 11. There is a landing to the right just beyond the bridge. It is about **.5 mile** from the twin bridges to the landing.

Road directions to the landing from River Bend Park (your launch place) are as follows: Take State Route 706 east to U.S. 1. Turn left. The entrance to Burt Reynolds Park, with the Florida History Center and Museum, will be on your right, within .5 mile.

Where to Eat & Where to Stay

RESTAURANTS Stroll across the road from *Paja Villas Motel* to *Schooners*, an excellent fish restaurant (1001 North A1A Ocean Boulevard, Jupiter, FL 33477; 651–746–7558), or try one of the other restaurants down the road. A short drive north will take you to a particularly good Thai restaurant, *Thai Lotus*, at Tequesta Shoppes (137 North U.S. 1; 407–743–0069). **LODGINGS** For a special experience of Florida, try the *Paja Villas Motel*, 18265 North A1A Ocean Boulevard, Jupiter, FL 33477; (561) 746–3881. It is just south of the U.S. 1A road bridge over Jupiter Inlet. Driving south, take the first left (east) after the bridge by Smiling Jack's Marina. This is Ocean Boulevard. The motel is a few yards farther on your right, opposite Schooners restaurant. **CAMPING** Camping is available at *Jonathan Dickinson State Park*, entrance to the west side of U.S. 1, 5 miles north of Jupiter. The park requires full payment with reservation and is booked up to eleven months in advance (561–546–2771).

Trapper Nelson

Vincent Nelson, the son of Polish immigrants, arrived in Florida at a time when trapping game was profitable. When game became scarce near Jupiter Inlet, he moved up the Loxahatchee River and in 1930 established the camp that remains today, close to what is now the tidal limit. He spent all the money he earned, buying up land around the camp. He lived on stews made from gophers and raccoons, and planted citrus trees to harvest the fruit. He was regarded as a romantic figure and was known to roam the jungle, dressed in shorts, a large bandanna tied around his head. As the story goes, he also delighted in swinging Tarzan-like from a rope hanging above the river.

Trapper Nelson became a tourist attraction. Cruise boats motored upstream to his dock to offload passengers. To entertain the tourists, Trapper built shelters and picnic tables and filled enclosures with wildlife he caught: alligators, snakes, turtles, and bobcats.

When Trapper Nelson died of gunshot wounds in 1968, many of his friends thought he'd been murdered; he'd been feuding with neighbors for years. However, his death was officially attributed to suicide. His own shotgun had been found nearby.

The state has now acquired much of the land. If you take the time to stroll around the camp, with its now-protected gopher turtles and empty animal enclosures, you can imagine what his life must have been like in the mid-twentieth century.

Route 2:

■ ■ ■ ■ ■ ■ ■ ■ ■ ■ ■ ■ ■ ■ ■ ➤

Jupiter Intracoastal Waterway

T his relaxing route highlights the contrast between the Old Florida, with secluded mangrove channels and tiny sandy beaches, and the typical Florida east coast dredge-and-fill canal development with parks, golf courses, and sumptuous architect-designed properties backing onto deepened waterways. Although I actually enjoy this particular route, it signifies why most of the routes in this guide are either on the west coast or in the Florida Keys. Because much of the east coast of Southern Florida is the land of the private dock, the personal motor yacht, and the bug-screened swimming pool. Yet despite the huge numbers of recreational power vessels and the fenced sections of waterway, this is also an area where manatees are found.

On the east coast, development is accelerating at a crazy pace. Paddling this area I was acutely aware of the new road bridge under construction, the natural waterfront of mangrove and slash pine being ripped out to make way for further development, and the packing of new buildings into the remaining spaces along the waterfront.

TRIP HIGHLIGHTS: The world of secluded mangrove channels and hidden white beaches contrasted with Florida waterfront development.

TRIP RATING:
Basic: However, exercise caution.

TRIP DURATION: 1 to 2 hours; 3.25 miles.

SIDETRIP 1: Add 1 to 2 hours and 3.4 miles.

SIDETRIP 2: Add 12 miles round trip to the wildlife preserve, but you can travel farther or less far, as you choose.

NAVIGATION AIDS: Waterproof Charts #17; NOAA chart #11472.

TIDAL INFORMATION: The tide runs swiftly in and out through Jupiter Inlet and into the nearby waterways. You will almost certainly need to paddle against the tide at some point. Keep close to the shore for the weakest current, and farther out for the strongest current.

CAUTIONS: The boat docks in this area are generally supported on piles. Take care when paddling on the upstream side of such docks to avoid being washed underneath by the current. Jupiter Inlet itself is best avoided by kayakers. The inlet is notorious for its strong tide stream (faster than paddling speed), which can produce a very rough and confused sea in conjunction with surf conditions on the Atlantic, and for its fast boat traffic in the narrow entrance. Anglers along the shore only complicate matters. Take particular care during an outgoing tide.

TRIP PLANNING: Plan to be on the water around high tide when there is sufficient depth of water to complete the whole trip.

LAUNCH SITE: There is a public boat ramp and free parking at Burt Reynolds Park close to the Florida History Center and Museum. By road from either I–95 or the Turnpike at River Bend Park, follow State Route 706 east to U.S. 1. Turn left (north) and look for the entrance to Reynolds Park and the history center on your right. The boat ramp is at the opposite end of the parking area from the museum.

DIRECTIONS

On launching, turn left and follow the channel for **.1 mile** under the low bridge to the Intracoastal Waterway. Turn right onto the waterway and after a **.25 mile**, turn right again into the Loxahatchee River.

You'll see a road bridge crossing the river in another **quarter mile** as you paddle east down the Loxahatchee. The red-painted stone tower of the Jupiter Lighthouse will be on your left as you emerge from beneath the bridge. (Sidetrip 2 begins from here.)

Hug the shore opposite the lighthouse as you paddle farther east. About **.5 mile** beyond the bridge, you'll come to a small park with picnic

Jupiter Intracoastal Waterway

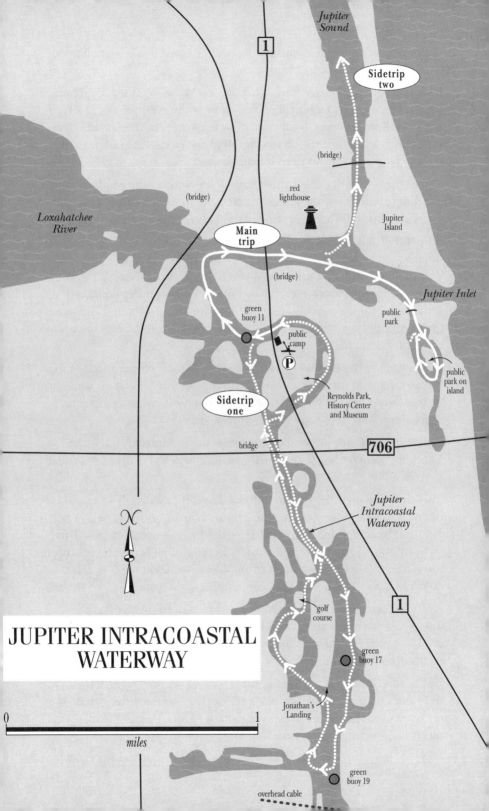

*Jupiter
Sound*

**Sidetrip
two**

(bridge)

red
lighthouse

*Jupiter
Island*

**Main
trip**

(bridge)

Jupiter Inlet

green
buoy 11

public
park

public
camp

P

public
park on
island

**Sidetrip
one**

Reynolds Park,
History Center
and Museum

bridge

706

*Jupiter
Intracoastal
Waterway*

N

golf
course

1

JUPITER INTRACOASTAL
WATERWAY

green
buoy 17

Jonathan's
Landing

0   1

miles

green
buoy 19

overhead cable

1

*Loxahatchee
River*

(bridge)

tables beneath some coconut palms, and just past this is a small inlet extending beyond a small bridge.

Paddle under the bridge and follow the creek between the sand banks for a **quarter mile** to a junction. You can continue either to the left or the right here, because both routes circle to meet at the far side of an island with a public park on it. Complete the circle (**.25 mile**), then retrace your route from here to your launch spot.

Once you've reached the Intra-coastal Waterway on the way back and are paddling south, look for the green channel marker 11 that is close to the creek on your left that leads under the bridge to your launch ramp.

SIDETRIP 1(**3.4 miles**): To extend your trip, continue south from channel marker 11, which is in the Intracoastal Waterway near the launch site. In less than **half a mile** you'll reach a bridge. The eastern shore from this bridge to as far as channel marker 17 (**.9 mile**) consists of a series of mangrove islands and channels through and under the mangrove canopy. A number of small, sandy beaches and islands rise above the high tide mark.

When you reach channel marker 19, cross to the western shore of the Intracoastal and turn back north again, just before you reach some overhead power lines. You'll pass a series of roped-off entrances to canals that offer a waterfront to exclusive properties.

Continue north for about a **quarter mile** until you reach Jonathan's Landing, named after Jonathan Dickinson, who was shipwrecked near here in 1696.

Turn into the channel past Jonathan's Landing marina. The entrance opens into a pool in which you might see marine patrol vessels at berth. Go straight ahead, past palm gardens, docks, and small bridges. Turn right when you reach the golf course. Beware of balls as you cross under the fairway. The function of the little paddleboat you see is to ferry golfers across the water so they can complete the course.

A left just after the golf course, followed by a right turn at the next junction, will return you to the Intracoastal Waterway. Turn left (north) onto the Intracoastal, and in **half a mile** you'll pass under the bridge you encountered outbound.

Just beyond the bridge, take the first channel on your right. This channel passes beneath a road bridge and loops around for **half a mile** to return you to the ramp that you launched from. (Coming from this direction, the ramp is on your left, just before the next bridge.)

Strange Encounter

I paddled this trip early one morning, leaving in the cool of first light. I was returning north along the Intracoastal Waterway, keeping close to shore. The sun was just rising through the trees, and a golden glare hit the water. In the shallows, I ran across what I thought was a log.

The water erupted around me as my kayak was lifted up and thrown onto one side, only to be lifted again, and then a third time. I braced wildly for balance, water streaming down my body as the manatee finally broke free from beneath the kayak and rushed toward deeper water.

I removed my sunglasses to shake the water from my hair before resuming what had been a peaceful and contemplative journey.

The Shipwreck

On August 23, 1696, the ship *Reformation* sailed from Jamaica, bound for Philadelphia. Twenty-six people were on board, including Jonathan Dickinson with his wife, his baby, and his eleven slaves. But far from their destination, the boat was caught in a storm and wrecked on the Florida coast, about 5 miles north of Jupiter Inlet.

The people managed to reach shore but were captured by Tequesta Indians, stripped of their clothing, and forced to return with the Indians to their village on top of an extensive shell mound at the south side of Jupiter Inlet. They finally persuaded the Indians to release them, and they were then able to make their way north, staying at Indian villages en route before being clothed again by Spanish sentinels.

They resumed their journey north, during which time several members of the party perished in the cold before the rest reached Charleston, South Carolina, just after Christmas. Their remarkable tale of endurance is recounted in *Jonathan Dickinson's Journal*, originally published in 1945 and now in print again in an edition from Florida Classics Library.

SIDETRIP 2 (**up to 12 miles**): This sidetrip extends the original route, beginning close to Jupiter Lighthouse on your way east. Keep Jupiter Lighthouse close to your left as you leave the Loxahatchee River and turn left to enter the Intracoastal Waterway, now traveling north. The tide can run swiftly though this channel and there is usually boat traffic, so hug the western shore unless the water becomes too shallow.

You will pass spectacular houses and several marinas on your left. Jupiter Island, to your right, is home to many millionaires, so after the first couple of miles, look for interesting architecture on the right bank.

After **5.5 miles** you will come to the start of a section of wildlife preserve on your left. Here is a good place to watch for anhingas, pileated woodpeckers, and ospreys. Manatees, too, are frequently seen here. This is a good place to relax for a while before turning around and paddling back.

Where to Eat & Where to Stay

For information on lodging, camping, and restaurants, see the section on where to eat and where to stay for Route 1, Loxahatchee River.

Route 3:

————————————————————▶

Egmont Key from Mullet Key

T his short but interesting trip starts on Mullet Key (south of St. Petersburg) and crosses Egmont Channel to Egmont Key. The channel not only features a tidal stream, but is also a shipping route for traffic traveling in and out of Tampa Bay.

Egmont Key is a National Wildlife Refuge, and has several points of interest including the Egmont Lighthouse, the remains of a civil war fort on the western shore, and gopher tortoises.

If you paddle a circuit of the island during the strength of the tidal stream, you'll probably experience steep breaking seas in the tide race off the northern point, particularly if the wind is against the stream. A similar tide race forms off the southern point.

TRIP HIGHLIGHTS: The transition from peaceful lagoon to exposed coast, the challenge of crossing a channel over a tidal stream, then the exhilaration of playing in a tide race (optional). Those different layers of experience—set against the relaxation of strolling across Egmont Key to view the lighthouse and the ruined fort, and watching gopher tortoises on the grass.

TRIP RATING:

Advanced: Because of the exposure of the crossing, the strength of the tide streams, and the certainty that big ships can appear and rapidly cross your path from either direction.

TRIP DURATION: Half day to full day; 6 to 11 miles. A basic round-trip measures about 6 miles. Add 4 miles if you make a circuit of Egmont Key. Add about 1.5 miles if you finish your trip by paddling around the northern tip of the barrier island beside

Mullet Key instead of portaging across. Allow half a day (about 4 hours) for the basic round-trip, including a stroll across Egmont Key. Allow a whole day for the full trip, with a relaxing lunch break on the island.

NAVIGATION AIDS: Waterproof Charts #22; NOAA chart #11417.

TIDAL INFORMATION: The ebb runs swiftly through Egmont Channel in a westerly direction (and northerly along the northern part of the eastern side of Egmont Key). A south-going eddy also forms along the west side of the southern tip of Mullet Key during the ebb. The floodtide runs southeasterly and easterly into Tampa Bay. Tide races form off the north and south tips of Egmont Key.

CAUTIONS: Be vigilant for shipping in the channel, which can be large and fast-moving. Cross the shipping channel at right angles, and do it quickly. The ebb tide runs north along the Egmont shore in the vicinity of the landing place. Aim to the south of your target, then drift with the tide to your landing to avoid being swept around the point into the tide race.

TRIP PLANNING: Plan to leave Mullet Key with at least two hours of ebb remaining so that you will get some tidal assistance. If you leave with four hours remaining, you'll probably get the greatest gain but the choppiest water. If you leave later, you run the risk of the tide turning against you before you reach Egmont Key.

LAUNCH SITE: At the northern end of the Sunshine Skyway bridge, (south of St. Petersburg), take Route 682 west for 2 miles, then Route 679 south. There is a toll payable on Pinellas Bayway

(Route 679) south only. At the T junction on Mullet Key, turn right. The road runs straight for a little more than a mile before bending north. You should see a large car park with shelters to your left after about a mile or so. This is Fort DeSoto County Park. Parking and launching is free. From the beach, look for a gap in the vegetation on the low, sandy barrier island just offshore. This is the portage point described in the trip directions.

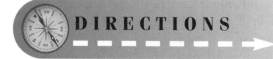

DIRECTIONS

Launch from Mullet Key in Fort DeSoto County Park, from the beach near the parking lot and pavilions. Paddle across the sheltered waterway (**.25 mile**) and portage the narrow sand beach of the barrier island to the Gulf coast. Egmont Key lies a little west of south, some **3 miles** distant.

Paddle along the beach to the southern point of Mullet Key until you can see your way clear of oncoming shipping from Tampa Bay (about **1.75 miles** from launch). Cross the shipping channel at right angles before aiming toward Egmont Key.

Note the strength and direction of the tidal stream as you cross toward Egmont. Typically a falling tide will sweep northwest around the northern tip of Egmont, so in this event aim for a central part of the island to avoid being carried around the northern point, and adjust your course when you are closer. The state of the sea will be noticeably rougher when any wind is against the tide. Mullet Key to Egmont Island is about **2 miles**.

Land on the beach adjacent to the small dock close to the northern tip of the east coast. Lift your kayak well clear of the shore, because the wake from passing ships occasionally sweeps the beach.

A paddling circuit of the island (**4 miles**) will carry you through any rough water that exists at either end of Egmont Key. Expect to spend 1.5 hours or more exploring the coast. It's prudent to land and stroll across the key to check out the sea state in the tide race from the top of the fort before you commit to paddling around the island.

Egmont Key from Mullet Key

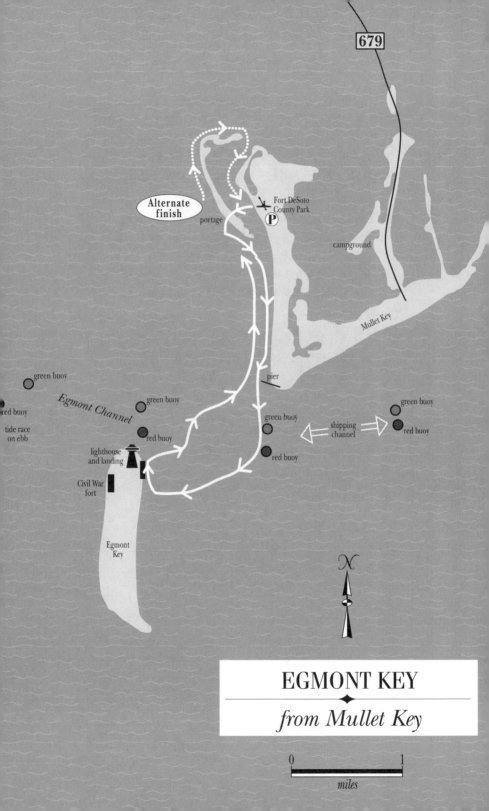

679

Alternate finish

portage

Fort DeSoto County Park

P

campground

Mullet Key

green buoy

Egmont Channel

green buoy

red buoy

tide race on ebb

red buoy

pier

green buoy

shipping channel

green buoy

red buoy

lighthouse and landing

red buoy

Civil War fort

Egmont Key

N

EGMONT KEY

from Mullet Key

0   1

miles

On Egmont Key

Follow the footpath from the dock inland to the lighthouse, to your right, and a grassy field, to your left. The burrows in the field are home for gopher tortoises, which may be seen foraging around the area.

The footpath continues to cross the island from close to the lighthouse, leading to the ruins of a Civil War fort and a good lookout over the Gulf. This spot affords an excellent view of the tidal race when it is running, with its clearly defined areas of fast-moving water (rougher) and slower eddies (calmer).

The fort was disguised by a ramp of sand and shell piled up against the western walls so that the aspect from the west would be one of a vegetated shoreline. This holds true to this day. The fort is almost invisible as you paddle around the island, even were it not for the distraction on rough days of the tide race around the northern point of the key.

Return to your launch site on Mullet Key in a fashion similar to your outward trip—that is, crossing the shipping channel at its narrowest, and following the Mullet Key coast northward back to the portage beach.

Either cross the portage beach and the narrow channel to the parking lot, or extend your trip by about **1.5 miles** by rounding the northern point of the barrier island to enter the shallow waterway from its only entrance.

Where to Eat & Where to Stay

R E S T A U R A N T S   *Billy's Stone Crab House* (727–866–2115). **L O D G I N G**   *Don Cesar's Resort*, a pink building by Pinellas Broadway, often used as a landmark (727–360–1181) or *Best Western St. Petersburg*, 5390 Gulf Boulevard, St. Petersburg (813–367–2771). **C A M P I N G**   There is a campground in the park (727–866–2662). Retracing your road route to the T junction on Mullet Key, the campground entrance lies about a mile north on the left, or west, of the road. The campground will not accept reservations by telephone— they must be made in person at the site.

Route 4:

▬ ▬ ▬ ▬ ▬ ▬ ▬ ▬ ▬ ▬ ▬ ▬ ▬ ▬ ▬ ▬ ➤

Egmont Key from Anna Maria Island

This trip includes a committing crossing of Passage Key Inlet to Passage Key and across Southwest Channel to Egmont Key. The tide passes through these channels and past the northern end of Egmont Key into and from Tampa Bay, which may make for rough conditions, particularly close to the points of land when the tide runs against any wind.

Passage Key is a National Wildlife Refuge popular as a resting area for flocks of wading birds and diving birds, including black skimmers and pelicans.

TRIP HIGHLIGHTS: Open crossings; waders and divers on Passage Key; the lighthouse, and Civil War fort on Egmont Key; tide races to surf off Egmont in suitable weather.

TRIP RATING:
Advanced: This can be an exciting trip.

TRIP DURATION: Full day trip; 9 to 10 miles.

NAVIGATION AIDS: Waterproof Charts #31 or #31E, or #21E (large-print waterproof); NOAA chart #1411.

TIDAL INFORMATION: Tides run swiftly in and out from Tampa Bay where the flow is restricted, especially near Egmont Key. The roughest tidal areas can be avoided by keeping half a mile to the east of Egmont as you approach until you are halfway along the island, and by avoiding the western side of the island during the ebb.

CAUTIONS: Conditions can change quickly. Pick a day when there are no storm warnings.

TRIP PLANNING: Make sure you have a compass and chart and are prepared for a 4-mile crossing. If you're after some rough water, and the opportunity to surf a small tide race, plan to arrive at Egmont during a spring tide with a westerly wind blowing. The race to the west of the north point builds on the ebb. Have a look from the top of the Civil War fort on Egmont before you go, but note that conditions will always look calmer from this viewpoint.

LAUNCH SITE: From Sarasota, take Route 789 north along the barrier keys from Lido Key to Anna Maria Island. Or, from U.S. 41 at Bradenton, take Route 64 west to Anna Maria Island. North of the junction with Route 64 on Anna Maria Island, Route 789 follows the western side of Anna Maria for about 2 miles, then turns right, crossing to the east. The municipal pier is ahead, and to the left are parking areas and a small beach suitable for launching.

DIRECTIONS

Leave Anna Maria on a bearing of about 340 degrees toward Passage Key, **1 mile** away. Adjust your course to the west to allow for drift with a flood tide, or to the east to allow for drift with an ebb tide.

Keep a couple of hundred yards distant as you pass Passage Key for half a mile to avoid disturbing any resting birds.

From Passage Key to Egmont Key, **1.4 miles**, follow a course of 320 degrees (adjust for drift).

Follow the eastern shore of Egmont for **1.5 miles** to the small pier close to the northern end and land on the beach in a sheltered spot on either side of the pier.

CAUTION: The wakes from ships navigating Egmont Channel to the north frequently wash the beach, so be sure to lift your kayak well onshore.

Egmont Key from Anna Maria Island

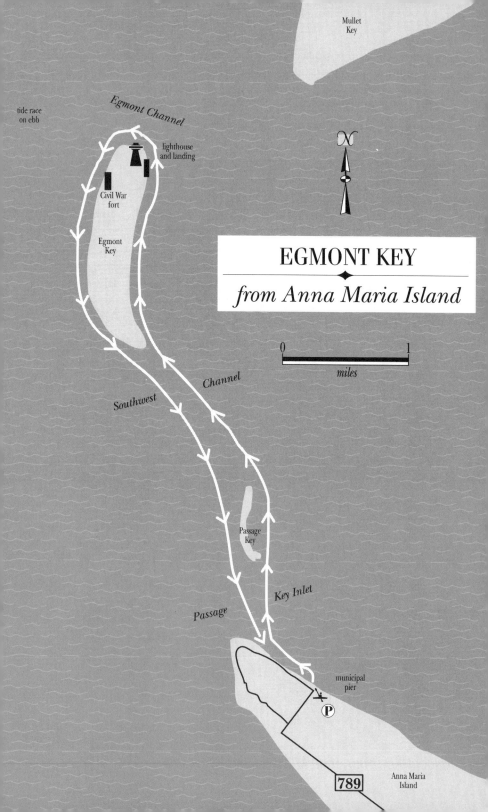

Mullet Key

tide race on ebb

Egmont Channel

lighthouse and landing

Civil War fort

Egmont Key

EGMONT KEY

from Anna Maria Island

0   1
miles

Southwest   Channel

Passage Key

Key Inlet

Passage

municipal pier

P

789   Anna Maria Island

Follow the footpath from the pier to the nearby lighthouse. From here, the footpath crosses the island to the ruins of a Civil War fort and a good lookout over the Gulf.

You have a choice of homeward journey: to retrace your outward journey or to continue around the northern tip of Egmont and down the western side.

CAUTION: A tide race develops around the north of the island at some states of the tide. You can check out conditions around the point from the top of the Civil War fort.

From the pier to the south end of Egmont via the west coast is **2 miles**; via the east coast is **1.5 miles**.

From the south end of Egmont, a bearing of around 160 degrees will take you back to Anna Maria Island, passing to the west of Passage Key, a total distance of about **2.5 miles**. Follow Anna Maria for **a half mile** to your launch beach (by the municipal pier).

Where to Eat & Where to Stay

RESTAURANTS *Beach Bistro*, close to the Gulf Beach Inn, is at 6600 Gulf Drive, Palm Beach, FL 34217 (941–778–6444). Also try *Rotten Ralph's* on State Route 64 (941–746–3097). For something very special, take a trip to *Morel*, 3809 South Turtle Avenue, Sarasota, FL (941–927–8716). It's well worth the drive, but you'll need to make reservations. **LODGINGS** Facilities include the *Gulf Beach Inn*, on the beach, at 101 66th Street, Anna Maria, FL 34217 (941–778–9597), and *Haley's Motel*, off the beach, at 8102 Gulf Drive, Holmes Beach, Anna Maria, FL 34217 (941–778–5405).

Route 5:

━ ━ ━ ━ ━ ━ ━ ━ ━ ━ ━ ━ ━ ➤

Lido Key

Lido Key is one of the islands that enclose Sarasota Bay close to the southern end. Although Lido Key is accessible by road, this trip begins on Siesta Key to enhance the island experience by adding the short return crossing of Big Sarasota Pass to the circuit of Lido Key. A small wildlife refuge and park occupies the southern end of Lido Key, with a park recreation beach bordering the Pass and mangrove tunnels to explore extending behind.

At the northern end are the twin attractions of the Pelican Man bird rehabilitation center and Mote Marine Laboratory and Aquarium, a marine research station. Both are open to the public, making this a great place to stop midway through the trip to get a close-up view of many species of local birds and of the sea life that often lurks somewhere beneath your kayak when you paddle—including sharks, barracuda, manatees, and turtles.

I enjoyed drifting on clear water in the evening light, past the end of the bathing beaches on the western side of Lido Key and out into Big Sarasota Pass, looking down at the dark shapes of rays swimming across the sandy bottom.

The offshore sandbank on the south end collects swells and boat wakes and heaps them into fun surfing waves larger than elsewhere in the area.

TRIP HIGHLIGHTS: The combination of traveling by kayak to Lido Key and seeing the wildlife at Mote Marine and Pelican Man.

TRIP RATING:

Basic/intermediate: The crossing of Big Sarasota Pass can add to the seriousness of the trip, but when conditions are rough on the Gulf side of the island, you can return via the sheltered side. This trip also includes a longer, more-advanced option.

TRIP DURATION: 2.5 to 3 hours; about 6 miles. Add 1.5 hours and 4 miles for the longer route. Allow at least another couple of hours for visits to Pelican Man and Mote Marine.

NAVIGATION AIDS: Waterproof Charts #21E; NOAA chart #11425.

TIDAL INFORMATION: The tide floods into and ebbs from the southern end of Sarasota Bay through the passes. On the longer alternative, the tide is weakest close to the shore and increases farther offshore, so keep close to shore if the stream is against you.

CAUTIONS: The passes can be busy with small boat traffic. If so, wait for a suitable opportunity, then cross straight over the marked channel without delay.

TRIP PLANNING: Take a cable and lock for attaching your kayak to a tree while you explore Mote Marine ($8.00 adult admission fee) and Pelican Man (free, but donations are requested). Shoes and shirt are required at both of these places, so I recommend a dry set of clothes to change into.

LAUNCH SITE: From U.S. Highway 41 (Tamiami Trail), take Siesta Drive west over the bridge onto Siesta Key. Look for the street sign for North Shell Road, a small side street to your right. Parking is free but limited. Launch from the small, sand North Shell beach for the shorter and more sheltered of the two routes described below. For the longer and more advanced route, continue farther, turning right toward Siesta Village along Ocean Boulevard. Pass through the village until a sharp left bend in the road. Free parking is available by the beach on your right at the bend. Launch from the Siesta Village beach.

DIRECTIONS

The two main trip alternatives follow the same route around Lido Key, but start from different places.

LAUNCH FROM NORTH SHELL BEACH (starting point for shorter trip; basic/intermediate): Paddle straight across Big Sarasota Pass to the eastern end of Lido Key as viewed from the shore (**.6 mile**).

CAUTION: Boat traffic uses this pass, so pick your time for crossing to coincide with a lull in activity if the channel is busy, and don't linger in the boat channel. Your target is the mangrove area to the east of the beach.

LAUNCH FROM SIESTA VILLAGE BEACH (starting point for longer trip; more advanced): Launch from the sand beach and turn right to paddle north along the popular tourist beach to the entrance of Big Sarasota Pass. The clearly marked boating channel lies close to the Siesta Key shore, so cross it directly to the offshore sandbank beyond the channel (**1 mile**). Continue across the pass to the southern shore of Lido Key, and follow the shore east to the southeastern corner (**1.75 miles**).

Both routes join at the southeastern corner of Lido Key. South Lido Beach Preserve, the wildlife refuge here, encompasses a small area of mangrove dissected by many narrow channels roofed over with mangrove. Allow about half an hour to explore these tunnels.

Of interest here are the many mangrove crabs—seen as shiny black lumps on the mangrove tap roots—that seem to slide out of sight as you approach closely. Oysters aggregate around the lower parts of the tap roots, and sponges encrust both the roots and the bed of the channel.

Paddle north from the wildlife refuge. A bridge crosses from Sarasota to Lido Key about halfway along the eastern shore (about **1 mile**). Beyond the bridge, aim for the northeast extremity of the island. You'll see a beach to your left after about a mile (about **.25 mile** before the point), with picnic tables beneath pine trees. Here is a good place to land for a visit to the nearby marine laboratory and aquarium and the bird rehabilitation center, which are situated near the beach.

From the northeast point of Lido Key (**.25 mile**), continue around the shore into New Pass, which runs between Lido and Longboat Keys. Two restaurants on your left offer a place for refreshments or snacks

Lido Key

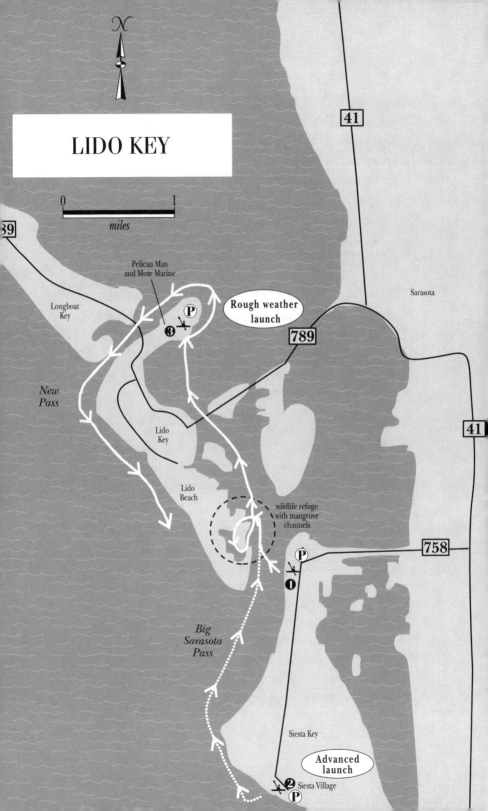

LIDO KEY

N

0   1
miles

39

Longboat
Key

New
Pass

Pelican Man
and Mote Marine

P

❸

Rough weather
launch

789

Sarasota

41

41

Lido
Key

Lido Beach

wildlife refuge
with mangrove
channels

758

P

❶

Big
Sarasota
Pass

Siesta Key

Advanced
launch

❷ Siesta Village

P

Meet the Creatures

Be sure to stop at the northeast end of Lido Key for a visit to the marine research station, Mote Marine, and to the bird rehabilitation center, Pelican Man. (Cable your kayak to a tree before walking away.)

Mote Marine covers two sites. The building with the Andrew Wyeth mural of an underwater scene (which features a pelican in the scene as a mark of respect for the work of Dale Shields, the "Pelican Man") houses turtles and manatees. The other building, closer to Pelican Man, contains an impressive tank flanked by underwater viewing windows through which you can watch some of the larger fish, including sharks and barracuda. There are other educational displays, including "touch tanks"—but the touch tanks don't contain sharks! Sharks live in the 135,000-gallon shark tank. Mote Marine Laboratory and Aquarium offers an opportunity to learn something of the wildlife that is beneath your kayak as you paddle in Southern Florida, and as a major research station is staffed by scientists who are leaders in various aspects of marine biology. There is an entrance fee of $8.00 for adults.

Dale Shields, "Pelican Man," cares for many birds too badly injured to be returned to the wild, although many recover and are released. He first began nursing injured pelicans to health; now the center cares for all species. I enjoyed the opportunity to look closely at herons and egrets, cranes and storks, gulls and terns that I typically view from my kayak at a greater distance This is a superb way to become familiar with characteristics that will make identification in the wild much easier. An entrance donation is encouraged.

before you reach the bridge over New Pass (**.5 mile** from the northeast point of Lido). The tide can funnel swiftly through the pass.

The western shore of Lido Key (**.5 mile** from the bridge) is white sand, with the classic translucent green water that is typical of the area in calm weather. Continue to the southern end and cross Big Sarasota Pass to your original launching beach (**1.75 miles** down the western shore and back to North Shell Beach; **4.25 miles** down the western shore and back to Siesta Key Beach).

ROUGH-WEATHER ALTERNATIVE (**5-mile** round-trip): Don't cross Big Sarasota Pass. Instead, begin your trip from the beach at the northeast tip of Lido Key and paddle south on the west side of the island to the wildlife refuge to explore the mangrove tunnels (**2 miles**). Land on the beach of the park on the south end of the island for a picnic lunch (**.5 mile**), then return the way you came. Back at the northeast tip of the island, you might continue your day with a visit to Mote Marine or Pelican Man before finishing at Old Salty Dog for a sandwich or fish and chips (on the waterfront adjacent to the marina on New Pass).

Where to Eat & Where to Stay

RESTAURANTS A stroll along Ocean Boulevard in Siesta Village will reveal the *Patisserie Cafe Continental*, a friendly European-style spot specializing in coffees, breakfast, and lunch, with almost everything baked on the premises. You'll find the patisserie on the east side of the street, set back and up steps from a parking area, at 5221 Ocean Boulevard, Unit 6, Siesta Key, Sarasota (941–346–3171). *Fandango's* (941–346–1711), at 5148 Ocean Boulevard, is on the west side of the street. This Siesta Key restaurant is excellent for a special meal. Fandango's features live music at least one evening per week. Lunches are also served here. **LODGINGS** In Siesta Village, the *Tropical Breeze Inn*, 140 Columbus Boulevard/Avenida Navarra, Siesta Key, FL 34242, offers some of the nicest accommodations in the area and is in easy walking distance of the beach and the best dining options (800–300–2492 or 941–349–1125; e-mail tropical.breeze@netsrq.com). Book ahead for winter reservations. Or try the *Best Western Siesta Beach Resort* at 5311 Ocean Boulevard, Sarasota, FL 34242 (800–223–5786 or 941–349–3211).

The Flamingo

It was a bright day. Scott and I launched from Siesta Key into small waves. They broke across my deck and against my body, tingling cool against sun-hot skin. We left the sunbathers and made for the sandbank out in the middle of the entrance to Big Sarasota Pass. Waves usually show up here, if only from passing boats, and today was no exception. The crystal ridges curved and steepened as they converged on the strip of exposed sand, moving bright lines of light and shifting shadows on the sand beneath us—liquid color, like thick glass, that intensifies sapphire to emerald with the depth of the water. We each caught a wave and surfed toward the pass.

Scott pulled abruptly off his wave and stopped. I wondered if something was wrong, but then I realized he was looking at a bird on the sandbank: a flamingo, with a fiery pink, almost red head paling downward into coral. The flamingo stepped with a curiously cautious gait, as if self-conscious about its color, then paused, heavy head reaching far down to the sand while it scooped with its feet, its pink red vibrant against the background of yellow sand, sea greens, and blues.

Route 6:

Turtle Beach

This is a relaxing cruise around the sheltered waterways inshore of the northern end of Casey Key and the southern end of Siesta Key, in the area still marked on many maps as Midnight Pass. Sandbanks and mudflats, mangrove islands and shallows provide a rich feeding ground and a sheltered nesting and roosting haven for wading and diving birds. Although I describe a route through the area, I recommend you take time to explore all the little channels that branch off between the small islands. In rough weather this area provides a welcome retreat, where you can paddle in shelter.

TRIP HIGHLIGHTS: Wild birds, and the possibility of finding fossil shark teeth on the Gulf beach.

TRIP RATING:
Basic: Easy paddling.

TRIP DURATION: One hour; 2.8 miles. For bird-watching, plan to spend at least two hours. Add extra time to search for fossil shark teeth on the beach. This trip also includes an option for additional paddling.

NAVIGATION AIDS: Waterproof Charts #21E; NOAA chart #11425.

TIDAL INFORMATION: The tidal range is small, but at low tide much of the area becomes too shallow to explore. Plan your trip to span high water, although a low-tide trip will reveal wading birds in action, with divers resting on the sandbanks. The divers favor a high tide, when the waders generally retreat into the mangroves.

CAUTIONS: Certain islands are favored as nesting sites by pelicans, herons, and egrets. Please keep your distance to avoid disturbing the birds.

TRIP PLANNING: The waters are shallow, and a pair of polarized sunglasses will help you see fish here.

LAUNCH SITE: Follow Route 789 toward the southern tip of Siesta Key. Neville Wildlife Park and Turtle Beach lie on your right just before the end of the road. There is a parking area (no fee) close to the end of a canal, into which you can launch (no fee). Note any restrictions on the notice board near the park entrance.

DIRECTIONS

From the end of the canal, paddle south past houses and condominiums. Herons and egrets seem to have staked out feeding territories in the gardens here, and you'll almost certainly see pelicans sitting on dock posts. It should take about fifteen minutes of paddling to reach a junction in the waterway (**.5 mile**).

Take a look at the two blocks of condominiums on your left when you reach this junction. Your route will take you in a counterclockwise circle from this point, returning toward these two buildings from the north. Recognizing them will help you locate the entrance to the canal when you return.

Paddle south (right) in shallow water. Just around a vegetated point to your right is a small bay, with the remains of concrete structures that were once holding tanks for sharks as part of a former marine research station.

A few yards ahead is a sandy beach (**.3 mile** from the condominiums), where Midnight Pass (now blocked) used to run out into the Gulf. From this beach, keep the mangrove islands to your left as you approach the Intracoastal Waterway, with its channel markers. A bay beyond the point

Turtle Beach

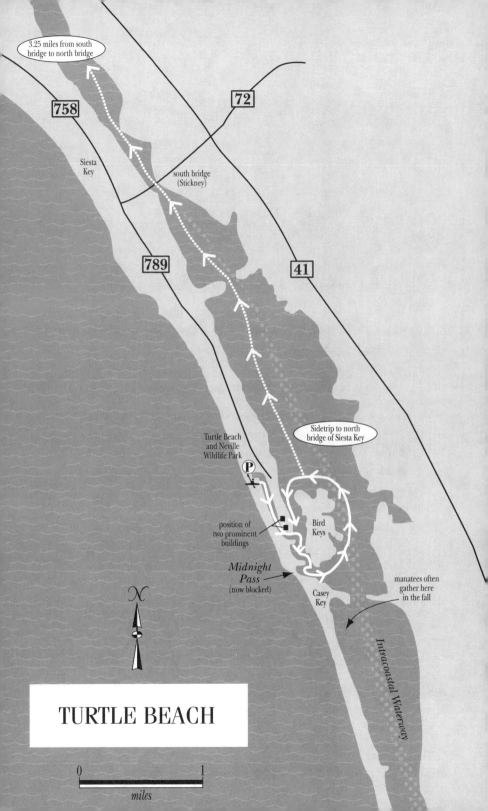

3.25 miles from south
bridge to north bridge

758

72

Siesta
Key

south bridge
(Stickney)

789

41

Turtle Beach
and Neville
Wildlife Park

P

Sidetrip to north
bridge of Siesta Key

position of
two prominent
buildings

Bird
Keys

*Midnight
Pass*
(now blocked)

Casey
Key

manatees often
gather here
in the fall

Intracoastal Waterway

N

TURTLE BEACH

0 1

miles

A Pass That Is No More

Midnight Pass used to be the preferred route in this area for local fishing boats to get from the Intracoastal Waterway and out into the Gulf of Mexico. Locals tell me the pass was illegally closed with the use of heavy earthmoving equipment under cover of darkness and immediately preceding a big storm. Closure of the channel was officially blamed on the storm itself.

Whatever the politics of the issue, the closure means boats now have to travel 6 miles south or 8 miles north to reach open water. The other result is the silting up of what is now a backwater, creating a superb nature reserve.

You can land at Midnight Pass beach and cross the sand to view the open sea. Scour the shoreline here and you're almost certain to find small, gleaming, black fossil shark teeth.

to the south is a gathering place for manatees in the fall when water temperatures begin to drop more quickly elsewhere.

You will see houses across the waterway. Keep the mangrove islands to your left. Keep your distance from the island obviously heavily used for nesting, with guano-stained foliage and a lot of birds.

A marked channel lies ahead. Continue to keep the mangroves to your left, and you will curve around into a channel with sandbanks between you and a boating channel that runs close to the buildings opposite. Ahead you should be able to recognize the two condominium blocks that identify the entrance to the canal where you started (**1.5 miles** from the Midnight Pass beach.) Complete your trip by returning to the end of the canal (**.5 mile**).

Now that you have paddled around the outside of this area, explore some of the delightful channels between the mangroves. You should be able to recognize your location wherever you might exit these channels.

SIDETRIP: The Intracoastal Waterway extends northwest about **6 miles** from the entrance to the Turtle Beach canal to the north bridge of Siesta Key. Island groups within this waterway make for good exploration. Your route will take you beneath the south bridge at Stickney Point (**2.75 miles**) and as far as the north bridge (**3.25 miles** beyond Stickney Point bridge), a good point for turning around. If you have a vehicle to pick you up, you may wish to pass under the north bridge and follow the shore around to land at the North Shell beach (see Route 5, Lido Key, for travel directions to North Shell Beach).

Where to Eat & Where to Stay

For lodging and restaurants, see the section on where to eat and where to stay for Route 5, Lido Key.

Route 7:

━━ ━━ ━━ ━━ ━━ ━━ ━━ ━━ ━━ ━━ ━━ ━━ ━━ ➤

Myakka River

The Myakka River winds through Myakka River State Park, passing through two lakes. It offers one of the finest opportunities to observe alligators in abundance. The river is freshwater and flanked by grassy marshes and oak and palm hammocks. Many bird species are at home here, including the huge sandhill crane and the limpkin.

We'll look at two routes. The Upper Route starts at the upper lake launching ramp and finishes at the southern entrance to the park, taking in a circuit of the upper lake and a descent of part of the river.

The Lower Route descends the Myakka River from the southern entrance to the park and encircles the lower lake before returning upstream to the starting point.

A well-planned weekend could include both kayak trips, plus additional activities. Hiking trails wind through the park. Bikes, canoes, and kayaks can be rented at the concession at the upper lake. There are boat tours on the upper lake, and tram tours with information about the wildlife.

TRIP HIGHLIGHTS: Quiet cruising on freshwater surrounded by lush vegetation, and the opportunity to watch birds and alligators.

TRIP RATING:
Basic/intermediate: Attractive to all levels of paddlers.

TRIP DURATION: A strong paddler can complete both routes in a day, but each makes a good full-day trip. The Upper Route is about 9 miles, and the Lower Route is about 6 miles.

NAVIGATION AIDS: USGS 1:24,000 topographic maps "Old Myakka Lake" and "Lower Myakka Lake."

TIDAL INFORMATION: No tide. The current on the river will vary depending on rainfall, so check the rate at the site.

CAUTIONS: Alligators are wild animals, and your safety depends on treating them as such. Be wary if you land at any point other than the designated launch sites. Many of the obvious beaches are alligator haul-outs. Please, no swimming! And on an unusual note: The park warns that vultures at upper Myakka Lake have developed a taste for window moldings and other vehicle trim. They recommend you avoid parking at the lake area before 10:00 A.M. to limit the chance of damage.

TRIP PLANNING: If doubtful of your ability to paddle upstream against the current, then choose the Upper Route, which is all downstream, instead of the Lower Route, which includes a return trip upstream.

LAUNCH SITE: From I–75, take State Route 72 east for 8.5 miles toward Arcadia. The south entrance to the park is on your left. The park is open from 8:00 A.M. till sundown daily. A park entrance fee is payable, but there are no additional parking or launching fees. Ask here for a pamphlet with a map to guide you to the upper lake.

The parking lot immediately inside the south entrance and to your right is the one for the Lower Route. You'll portage across the grass to the river from the far end of the lot.

For the Upper Route, drive along the park road and take the left fork to the boat basin and its parking lot. Launch into the lake at the ramp at the parking lot.

DIRECTIONS

UPPER ROUTE: Follow the shore of the lake, to your left, after launching to find where the river runs out from the lake. Next, explore all or part of the lake before you begin your river descent.

A full circuit of the lake measures a little more than 6 miles. If you cross the river entrance and explore the shore beyond, you'll find a peaceful area of hidden creeks tucked away into the shoreline in a manner that defies observation until you are right there. These creeks offer a wonderful retreat from the lake, and good sheltered exploration in windy weather. There are more hidden creeks at the far side of the lake. Enjoy this opportunity to explore.

The Myakka River meanders downstream from the lake through marshy grassland for about **3 miles.** Be alert for alligators and wading birds, which can be seen on the banks. Your route will pass beneath the park road. Your exit point near the park entrance will be on your right, among trees. Look for picnic tables and shelters. If you reach the main road bridge on State Route 72, you have gone too far.

A short portage from the landing, across grass, will bring you to the south entrance parking lot.

LOWER ROUTE: From the launch area by the south entrance parking lot, paddle downstream to the lower lake (**1 mile**). Be watchful of alligators basking on the banks or floating at the surface. We saw dozens, ranging in size up to more than 12 feet. The shores are lined with marshy grassland on some stretches and woodland with palm and live oak along others.

When you reach the lower lake, note the exit you took from the river. There are sometimes several options, depending on the water level, and you will need to find your way back.

The lower lake is divided **1.5 miles** from the upper river entrance by spits extending from either shore. Choose here whether you wish to explore the more wooded shore of the second section of the lake, or to make the short crossing to circle the upper part of the lake only. A full circuit of the lake measures about **4.5 miles.**

The return upriver can appear confusing at high water levels when the current in side branches of the river is almost as great as that in the river

-52-   *Myakka River*

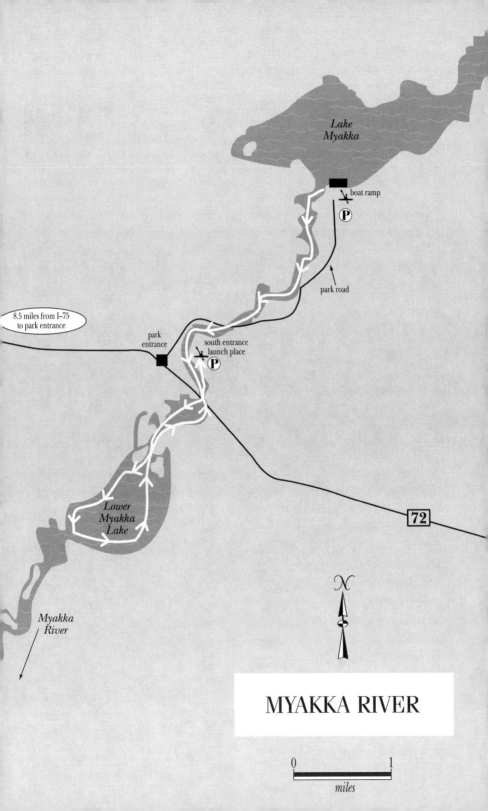

Lake
Myakka

boat ramp

Ⓟ

park road

8.5 miles from I–75
to park entrance

park
entrance

south entrance
launch place

Ⓟ

72

Lower
Myakka
Lake

Myakka
River

N

0   1
miles

MYAKKA RIVER

itself. Pick the strongest current in each case. Your exit, back at the south entrance, is preceded by the Route 72 bridge, so you can tell when you're almost back.

Where to Eat & Where to Stay

RESTAURANTS No recommendations. **LODGING AND CAMPING** Camping facilities and fully furnished log cabins are available in the park (941–361–6511; e-mail myakka@ix.netcom.com).

Alligators

Alligators are not normally dangerous unless they become accustomed to people, especially if they associate people with food. But mother alligators are very protective of their young, guarding them for more than a year. If you hear young alligators squeaking or whimpering, make a rapid retreat. The mother will be much larger, much faster, and may be extremely aggressive. You may spot groups of young alligators clustered on riverbanks or at the edges of waterways. Do not be tempted to creep closer for a look!

As an alligator floats in the water, you'll usually see its nostrils and eyes protruding above the surface. You'll probably also see the pattern of its armored skin along the back, looking rather like a floating palm log. You almost never get a true impression of the bulk of an alligator when it's floating. But as a rough guide to its length, an alligator will be about the same number of feet long as the distance in inches between eyes and nostrils. But I don't recommend you use a tape measure!

Route 8:

▬ ▬ ▬ ▬ ▬ ▬ ▬ ▬ ▬ ▬ ▬ ▬ ▬ ▬ ▬ ▬ ➤

Peace River: Zolfo Springs to Gardner

The Peace River rates doubly as a peaceful river and a place of excitement. If you're not careful, you can become intoxicated like a Klondike gold-digger by the search for hidden treasure! The Peace River is not noted for its gold, but its golden-colored, tannin-rich waters do run through ancient limestone, dissolving fragile sediments and releasing fossils that have been trapped there since the time of early mammals.

Never was fossil identification easier than here. The fossils all date from a single period after dinosaurs died out, when mammals such as the mastodon and mammoth roamed this area.

Some of the most commonly found fossils are shark teeth. One shark species now extinct, the giant version of the great white shark, had teeth the size of a human hand. When I sift through handfuls of river gravel and find myriad shark teeth, it makes me wonder about how densely populated with shark the seas may have been back then, before the days of sea kayakers.

The Peace River winds through palms and live oaks draped in Spanish moss, over rough limestone bedrock shallows and dark-stained gravels beds, passing groves of citrus trees bedded in poison ivy and sharp palmetto. You are as likely to see a river otter as an alligator. Kingfishers and anhingas feast on the fish that spawn in the sandy shallows.

The river lends itself to drifting, yet the distance between put-in and get-out necessitates some steady paddling if a one-way journey is to be made. The alternative is to head upstream, search for fossils, then allow the current to float you back to your put-in point. A shallow river level is best for fossil hunting, yet this will be harsh on a composite hull. For faster downstream cruising, choose higher water levels.

TRIP HIGHLIGHTS: A beautiful river descent, with the diversion of fossil hunting. For more information on fossil hunting, see Route 10, Peace River Fossil Hunt.)

TRIP RATING:
Basic

TRIP DURATION: A full day; 16 miles. The current will assist you. Wilderness camping is permitted along the west bank, except where you see NO TRESPASSING signs.

NAVIGATION AIDS: USGS topographic map 1:24,000, "Zolfo Springs" and "Gardner."

Snakes of Florida

The Florida National Parks Association says twenty-six species of snakes are found in Southern Florida parks including four that are venomous: the diamondback and pygmy rattlesnakes, the cottonmouth, and the coral snake.

Identification is not always easy at a glance. I was sitting at a table writing notes in a peaceful Florida cabin when I glanced up to see a large, dark snake moving steadily in through a gap in the screen door, only a few feet from where I sat. For a brief moment I considered how long it would take to fetch the snake book for a positive identification, but then decided that maybe I'd better just retreat. As I moved away, the snake took a similar action. It turned and slid out through the gap it had entered, and vanished into the undergrowth outside.

My subsequent "quick identification" proved to be a little more difficult than I'd expected. The snake may well have been an eastern indigo. If I'd known which features to look for, I might have been able to say for sure that it wasn't a cottonmouth, which can also sometimes appear similarly large and dark. The eastern indigo is harmless. The cottonmouth is not.

While paddling in Florida, I've seen many snakes—sometimes on riverbanks or curled in branches overhanging the water, once in a tangle of flood debris beside my head as I attempted to squeeze underneath. A good way to deal with snakes is to give them a wide berth, but you can only do that if you've spotted them first. So be observant.

TIDAL INFORMATION: Tides do not affect this river, but water level can vary. Low levels are best for finding fossils, higher levels are better for fast cruising with maximum assistance from the current.

CAUTIONS: At low water levels, the bedrock ledges and gravel banks can damage your hull. Beware of poison ivy on the banks.

TRIP PLANNING: Allow plenty of time for a transport shuttle. This is a trip that is easiest with two vehicles, or a non-paddling driver to handle drop-off and pickup. Allow a full long day; it is easy to get absorbed in fossil hunting at your get-out. A shuttle service is available through the Canoe Outpost (941–494–1215).

LAUNCH SITE: From U.S. 17 at Zolfo Springs, take State Route 64 west to the boat ramp at Pioneer Park, Zolfo Springs. A museum at Pioneer Park displays some spectacular fossils. The take-out spot is near Gardner, which is 10 miles south of Zolfo Springs on U.S. 17. Take the only road west (located immediately south of the junction between 17 and 665) from Gardner. You'll reach the exit boat ramp after 1.5 miles.

DIRECTIONS

Simply launch into the river and paddle downstream. The river is joined by numerous small streams, which may be difficult to identify in low water. Use the topographic map for detail, although there is little in the way of major landmarks until you reach the boat ramp at Gardner, **16 miles** from your starting point.

Where to Eat & Where to Stay

For information on lodging, camping, and restaurants, see the section on where to eat and where to stay for Route 9, Peace River: Gardner to Arcadia.

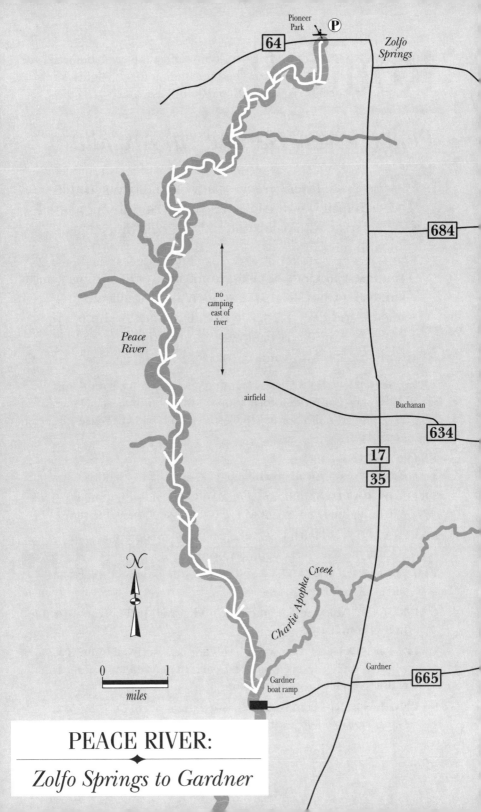

Pioneer
Park

P

64

*Zolfo
Springs*

684

no
camping
east of
river

*Peace
River*

airfield

Buchanan

634

17

35

N

Charlie Apopka Creek

Gardner

665

0 1

miles

Gardner
boat ramp

PEACE RIVER:
◆
Zolfo Springs to Gardner

Route 9:

━━ ━━ ━━ ━━ ━━ ━━ ━━ ━━ ━━ ━━ ━━ ━━ ➤

Peace River: Gardner to Arcadia

The Peace River here flows through limestone country
with many sandy banks. The route runs through wooded areas, with palms and with live oaks draped in
Spanish moss.

You'll see all kinds of birds, from vultures to anhingas and
kingfishers, but keep an eye open also for alligators,
snakes, and deer. Closer to Arcadia, there are homes by
the river, and the river slows—but the upper stretches
remain pleasantly wild.

TRIP HIGHLIGHTS: Fossil hunting and pleasant current-assisted
paddling. (For more information on fossil hunting, see Route 8,
Peace River: Zolfo Springs to Gardner, and Trip 10, Peace River
Fossil Hunt.)

TRIP RATING:
   Basic: No technical difficulties.

TRIP DURATION: 5 hours; 17 miles. Wilderness camping is permitted along the river except where you see NO TRESPASSING signs.

NAVIGATION AIDS: USGS 1:24,000 scale topographic maps—
"Gardner," "Nocatee," and "Arcadia."

TIDAL INFORMATION: No tides on river, but water levels can
vary.

CAUTIONS: At low water, limestone and gravel shallows can wear the
hull of your kayak.

TRIP PLANNING: Low water levels are best for fossil hunting,
whereas higher levels have faster current and offer a quicker run
with less contact with the bottom.

LAUNCH SITE: From Arcadia, drive 9 miles north on U.S. 17 to
Gardner. Turn left (west) on State Route 665. The launch site is

about 1.5 miles down the road. The take-out point at the end of the trip is in De Soto County Park by the old Arcadia road bridge, which runs alongside but upstream of the new Route 70 road bridge, just outside the outskirts of Arcadia to the west. Take Hickory Street in Arcadia west from U.S. 17. If you find yourself on the Route 70 bridge, continue past the junction with Route 72 and double back at the first junction on your right, which is the old road, the one you want. Canoe Outpost operates a shuttle service (941-494-1915)

Where to Eat & Where to Stay

RESTAURANTS The *Golden Coral* steakhouse (1119 East Oak Street, Arcadia, FL 34226; 941-494-5348) and the *Clock* restaurant (1121 East Oak Street, Arcadia, FL 34226; 941-494-4404) are both in Arcadia on Route 70 east. **LODGING** In Arcadia, choices include *Magnolia House* bed and breakfast (941-494-4299), *Parkerhouse* bed and breakfast (800-969-2499), and *Best Western* motel (941-494-4884). **CAMPING** Wilderness camping is permitted on the riverbanks unless there are NO-TRESPASSING signs. The *Arcadia Peace River* campground is close to the junction of Routes 70 and 72 near Arcadia (941-494-9693).

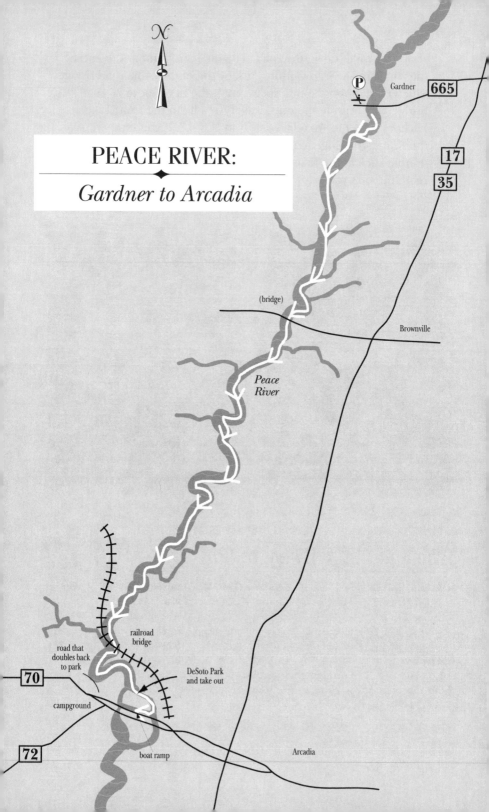

PEACE RIVER:

Gardner to Arcadia

N

P ⚲ Gardner 665

17

35

(bridge)

Brownville

*Peace
River*

railroad
bridge

road that
doubles back
to park

70

DeSoto Park
and take out

campground

72

boat ramp

Arcadia

D I R E C T I O N S

Take off from the Gardner boat ramp. After **6 miles**, you will go beneath the Brownville Road Bridge. After a further **10 miles**, a railroad bridge crosses the river. From here it's only about **1 mile** to the get-out at the end of your **17-mile** trip.

Route 10:

━ ▬ ━ ▬ ━ ▬ ━ ▬ ━ ▬ ━ ▬ ━ ▬ ━ ▬ ━ ▬ ━ ▬ ▶

Peace River Fossil Hunt

This is a short fossil-hunting trip, exploring upstream from the Gardner boat ramp. You can choose to paddle just as far upstream as you wish. Your return journey will be downstream and therefore easier than your upward journey.

The confluence of Charlie Apopka Creek and the Peace River, about a quarter mile upstream from the boat ramp, is considered a good place to find fossils, so there is no need to paddle far. Some people, however, consider the more inaccessible spots to be more promising.

TRIP HIGHLIGHTS: The excitement of the search for fossils! You will probably find many. The river is known for some spectacular finds: pieces of mammoth tusk, mastodon teeth, huge vertebrae, immaculate shark teeth. Visit the museum at Pioneer Park in Zolfo Springs, 10 miles north of Gardner, to see something of what has been found.

TRIP RATING:
Basic

TRIP DURATION: Half day to full day. The round-trip from Gardner boat ramp to Charlie Apopka Creek is only half a mile, but you can extend the trip as far as you wish.

NAVIGATION AIDS: USGS 1:24,000 scale topographic map "Gardner."

TIDAL INFORMATION: No tides on river, but water levels can vary. Fossil hunting is best at low water levels.

CAUTIONS: Please restrict your fossil hunting to the river bed and do not search on private land (including the river banks). Significant finds must be reported. Refer to *Florida's Fossils* (see appendix, page 222) for more details.

Fossil Treasures

The river was really low. The two of us headed upstream beneath the overhanging branches, picking the deeper water across the gravel banks and chasing across the deeper pools.

"Hey, look! Bet there's some stuff down in that 'gator hole," called Larry. I looked up to see Larry already wading across the river toward the trees on the other bank. The river suddenly went deep, but Larry kept right on going. Soon he was at the other side and calling me over: "Bring the strainer with you."

I followed, wondering whether the deep spot in the stream was indeed a 'gator hole, and what my chances were of being attacked by an alligator. The cold water rose higher up my thighs. I looked behind me for just a moment. When I looked around again, there was no sign of Larry. Vanished!

Moments later he reappeared, rising from the water, wearing his black face mask. In his hands were some pale objects that he was examining. Suddenly he lifted one high with a cry and urged me across to him. He'd picked up a vertebra some 10 inches across! His face was jubilant.

Then we got down to business—scooping gravel from the bottom, and sifting through it to select and set aside the best of the shark teeth, pieces of turtle shell, and bones. Then Larry brought up a scoopful of coarse gravel that changed a fun day to a truly memorable one.

There, sitting in the scoop of gravel, was a perfect mastodon tooth—5 inches long, 2 inches wide, and about 3 inches deep. Beautiful! Our whoops of excitement were suddenly stilled as our probing fingers uncovered a shark tooth nearly 3 inches long. Then we uncovered an Indian spearhead. Three treasures in a single scoopful!

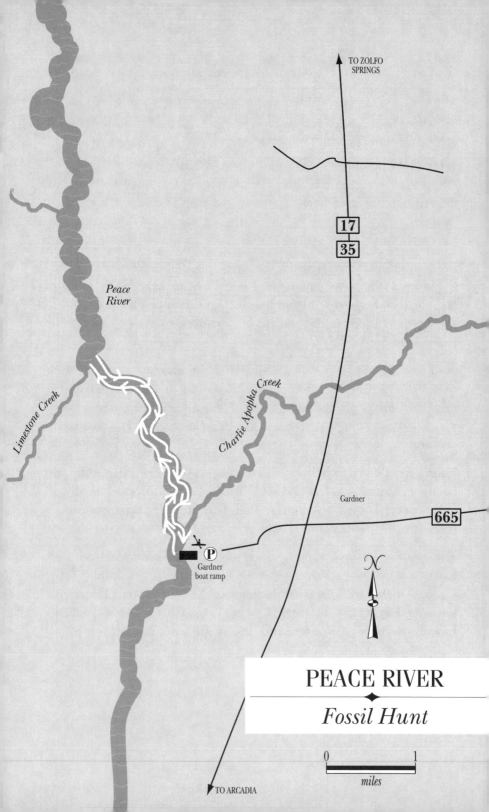

TO ZOLFO
SPRINGS

17
35

Peace
River

Limestone Creek

Charlie Apopka Creek

Gardner

665

Gardner
boat ramp

N

PEACE RIVER

◆

Fossil Hunt

0   1

miles

TO ARCADIA

TRIP PLANNING: Take some line to tether your kayak, as this is often easier than finding a suitable shore for beaching it. A small scoop and a strong mesh strainer will make your fossil-hunting more productive. Scoop gravel into the sieve to drain the water, then finger through the gravel to search for fossils. Wear shoes, and warm clothing, for wading the river.

LAUNCH SITE: Gardner boat ramp is situated 1.5 miles west of Gardner on Route 665. Gardner is approximately midway between Arcadia and Zolfo Springs on U.S. 17, about 9 miles from either.

DIRECTIONS

From Gardner boat ramp, paddle upstream just a **quarter-mile** to the confluence with Charlie Apopka Creek, which joins in from the right (east). If you keep left here, the next junction upstream with the Peace River is Limestone Creek, which joins in from the left (west). The junction with Limestone Creek is **3 miles** upstream from the boat ramp.

Where to Eat & Where to Stay

For information on lodging, camping, and restaurants, see the section on where to eat and where to stay for Route 9, Peace River: Gardner to Arcadia.

Route 11:

■ ■ ■ ■ ■ ■ ■ ■ ■ ■ ■ ■ ■ ➤

Boggess Hole

ur exploration of a part of Charlotte Harbor includes two trips: this one to Boggess Hole, and the next trip in the book, to Cape Haze.

These are both sheltered water trips in the shallow water of Gasparilla Sound and Island Bay in Charlotte Harbor. Advanced paddlers would find them interesting routes in almost any weather, and they're both ideal for beginners in calm weather. Much of the area is covered by water of knee deep or less, and is therefore never very rough. But because it is difficult to paddle when the water is too shallow to accommodate all of your blade, be cautious if the wind is from the west. A west wind will quickly carry you away from your launching place, but it may be difficult to work your way back.

The area is suitable for general exploration. Landing is limited, however, with much of the area an historic preserve, and most included in the Island Bay National Wildlife Preserve and Wilderness. Most of the area forbids trespassing. Mangrove islands and long creeks extend north into the peninsula. The area we will explore measures about 6 miles west to east and about 4 miles north to south, with the exception of a couple of longer creeks.

Calusa Indians built shell mounds in the area. These can be most easily identified by the elevation of the mounds—typically 8 to 20 feet higher than elsewhere—and by the different vegetation that grows on the higher and drier land. Gumbo limbo trees with their thin, papery, flaky bark, for example, thrive on the mounds, as do pines and palmettos. The mounds are constructed of banked-up shells, plus fire ash, shell tools, and pottery fragments. Shards of blackened orange clay pottery can be spotted on the beaches where erosion is eating into the mounds.

Launching into Placida Harbor for either route, you'll pass beneath the toll bridge that runs onto Gasparilla Island and also under a ruined bridge now used by anglers; then paddle eastward into an area of shallows, small islands, and mangroves. You'll likely see many small fish in this shallow water, and thus a thriving bird population.

We watched a school of dolphins herding fish into the shallows around us between the two bridges. Pelicans attracted by the fish were panicked into the air by the swift-cruising dolphins as they circled the shoals of fish.

TRIP HIGHLIGHTS: An intriguing area of shallow water and many small islands, with the water constantly moving with fish activity.

TRIP RATING:
Basic

TRIP DURATION: Full day; 8 to 9 miles.

NAVIGATION AIDS: Large-print Waterproof Charts #25E; NOAA chart #11426.

TIDAL INFORMATION: There is little tidal range, but because the water is so shallow, a drop of a few inches makes paddling more difficult.

CAUTIONS: The area offers some shelter in windy conditions, but shallow water makes for difficult paddling against the wind.

TRIP PLANNING: Ideally, plan to explore the area spanning high tide, especially during spring tides. When the water level drops in the shallow bay, paddling becomes increasingly hard work due to bottom drag and the difficulty of getting a full paddle blade into the water. The tide floods from the west and ebbs back to the west, so you'll get help if you paddle east with the last of the flood and west with the first of the ebb.

LAUNCH SITE: From U.S. 41 north of Port Charlotte, turn south on Route 771 to Placida. Follow the sign for Gasparilla Island, but pull in to your right at Elfred's Marina just before the toll for the causeway leading onto the island. Here you will see a sign advertising fishing tackle, live bait, and "live orchids." There is a ramp fee of $3.00, payable at the marina office.

DIRECTIONS

From the launch ramp, keep close to the left shore until you come in sight of the first bridge (**.5 mile**). Pass under this bridge. A second bridge, now used as a fishing pier, comes soon after.

CAUTIONS: Be careful when passing under the old bridge because of the danger of underwater posts—and overhead fishing lines. From here eastward are many scattered islands, each bearing a close resemblance to the next, so be careful with your map reading.

Paddle from the fishing bridge for **1 mile** to Catfish Point. Cross Catfish Bay in an easterly direction, passing south of any mangrove keys you encounter, but continuing east until you hit the mainland shoreline (**.5 mile**).

Follow this shore southeast, then east, for about **1 mile** until the entrance to Boggess Hole opens to the north as a narrow channel.

Follow this twisting channel for **three-quarters of a mile** until it widens into the broad but shallow pool known as Boggess Hole. The pool measures about half a mile across.

CAUTION: Some dead ends branch from the main channel, but none of them go far. But even the main channel is so shallow you may be forced to wade in some places.

Boggess Hole teems with shoals of mostly small fish, food for wading birds. The shores are posted "No Access" because of Calusa Indian shell mounds around the pool.

On your return journey from Boggess Hole, you can retrace your original path, or paddle southwest until you can see Catfish Point to then return across open but still-shallow water.

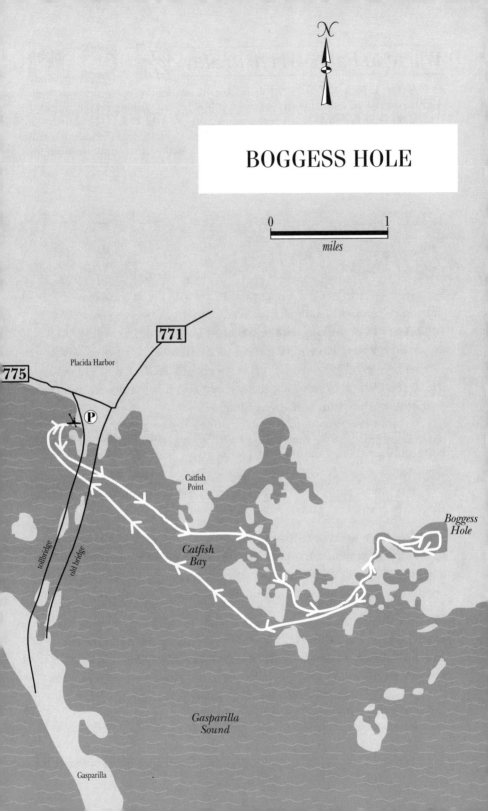

RESTAURANTS A fish restaurant sits by the water on your right shortly before you reach the first of the two bridges (the fishing bridge) on your return. **LODGING** No recommendation. **CAMPING** There is a campground at *Gasparilla Island State Park*, Boca Grande, near the southern end of Gasparilla Island. Take the road onto Gasparilla Island, then continue south for about 5 miles (941–964–0375).

Calusa Indians

Southern Florida has been occupied by people for at least twelve thousand years, with Calusa Indians dominant during the past thousand. They built temples and stilt homes on flat-topped mounds above high water. They were gatherers, hunters, and fishermen. For fishing they used gill nets, or fish traps constructed of shells piled in the shallow water from which they caught fish using dip nets. Line was fabricated from palm and yucca fiber.

Shell mounds are the most lasting evidence of widespread Calusa communities. Today the mounds, grown over with vegetation, are almost invisible. For the Calusa, the mounds provided dry ground as well as a way to dispose of the shells from the shellfish in their diet. Bones, fire ash, and pottery waste also went into the mounds.

The sites have been attractive to modern developers, who are drawn to the dry ground and the easy source of fill material for roadbeds and foundations. Many shell mounds have been destroyed, while others now sit almost untouched beneath houses.

Many of the mounds that have not already disappeared have been placed out of public reach in prohibited areas by the government. If you look closely at the shoreline in known areas of shell mounds, you may see pottery shards, especially where the bank of shell mound is being eroded by the sea. But however many fragments you may see scattered along the shore, collecting them is against the law.

Route 12:

Cape Haze

This trip is the second of our two trips exploring a part of Charlotte Harbor. The first was the trip to Boggess Hole that precedes this one in the book. These are both sheltered trips in the shallow water of Gasparilla Sound and Island Bay in Charlotte Harbor.

For further general information on both trips, read the introduction to Route 11, Boggess Hole.

TRIP HIGHLIGHTS: An intriguing area of shallow water and many small islands, with the water constantly moving with fish activity.

TRIP RATING:
   Basic: However, this trip will fascinate paddlers of all experience levels.

TRIP DURATION: Full day; 18 miles.

NAVIGATION AIDS: Large-print Waterproof Charts #25E; NOAA chart #11426.

TIDAL INFORMATION: There is little tidal range, but because the water is so shallow, a drop of a few inches makes paddling more difficult.

TRIP PLANNING: Ideally, plan to explore the area spanning high tide, especially during spring tides. When the water level drops in the shallow bay, paddling becomes increasingly hard work due to bottom drag and the difficulty of getting a full paddle blade into the water. The tide floods from the west and ebbs back to the west, so you'll get help if you paddle east with the last of the flood and west with the first of the ebb.

LAUNCH SITE: From U.S. 41 north of Port Charlotte, turn south on Route 771 to Placida. Follow the sign for Gasparilla Island, but pull in to your right at Elfred's Marina just before the toll for the cause-way leading onto the island. Here you will see a sign advertising fishing tackle, live bait, and "live orchids." There is a ramp fee of $3.00, payable at the marina office.

DIRECTIONS

Begin as for Route 11, Boggess Hole, following directions as far as the entrance to Boggess Hole (**3.5 miles** from the launch site).

Then continue in a generally easterly direction for another **3.5 miles**, keeping the mainland to the north and weaving a route through the small keys until you reach the western shore of Turtle Bay. Cross to the eastern side of the bay, about **three-quarters of mile**.

Cape Haze lies **2 miles** farther, at the southern extremity of the peninsula east of Turtle Bay. The cape affords views across the open water of Charlotte Harbor to land **5 miles** east and to Pine Island **5 miles** south.

It's worth spending some time exploring interesting inlets and channels in the mangroves around the end of Cape Haze.

Return by a more southerly route, crossing southwest from Cape Haze to Gallagher Keys. Keep open water to your left (south) until you pass Little Cape Haze, just over **4 miles** from Cape Haze. To the northeast of Little Cape Haze is Bull Bay, with a couple of houses on pilings—one of the houses with a huge osprey nest on the roof.

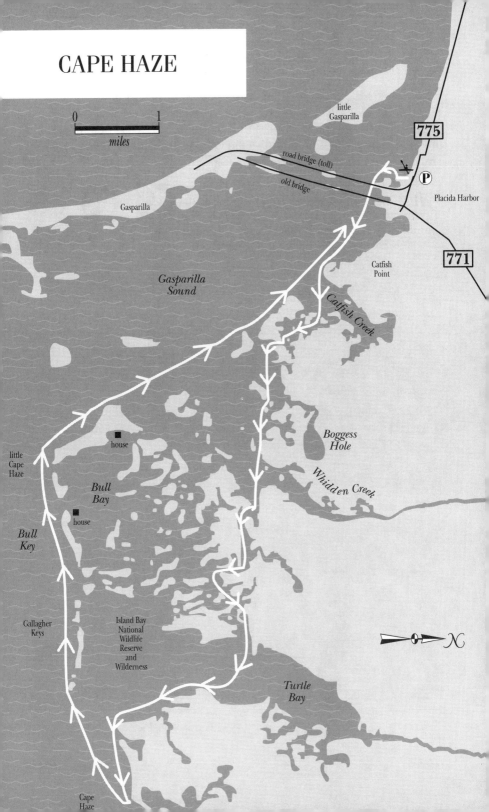

CAPE HAZE

0   1
miles

little
Gasparilla

775

road bridge (toll)

old bridge

P

Gasparilla

Placida Harbor

Gasparilla
Sound

771

Catfish
Point

Catfish Creek

Boggess
Hole

little
Cape
Haze

house

Whidden Creek

Bull
Bay

house

Bull
Key

Gallagher
Keys

Island Bay
National
Wildlife
Reserve
and
Wilderness

Turtle
Bay

N

Cape
Haze

Now turn northwest from Little Cape Haze and head back to your launch site, **5.25 miles** away at a bearing of 320 degrees.

If you're looking for more shelter on the return trip, travel on the north side (rather than the south side) of Gallagher Keys and the other islands. At no stage is a crossing more than three-quarters of a mile, but the multitude of small keys and shallows make it prudent to keep a general compass check backed up by line of sight where possible.

Where to Eat & Where to Stay

For information on lodging, camping, and restaurants, see the section on where to eat and where to stay for Route 11, Boggess Hole.

Route 13:
▬ ▬ ▬ ▬ ▬ ▬ ▬ ▬ ▬ ▬ ▬ ▬ ▬ ➤
Cabbage Key from Boca Grande

This one- or two-day round trip begins at Boca Grande and crosses Boca Grande Pass to Cayo Costa, an island. Here the shore is of the finest sparkling sand, extending in shallow bars and fine spits causing refracting waves that send interacting dancing patterns of shadows across the seabed. This is undeveloped coast, where you see dolphins and diving birds but few people. Tiny brown waders cling to the breeze and run along the shore. Here you'll see terns, black skimmers, and pelicans. It's easy to paddle along at a distance from the shore, but it pays to stay close. Clear sapphire water edges the sand where the backwash fingers iridescent shells.

A portage crosses the sand to a pool on the other side of Cayo Costa, where the water is as green as the reflected mangroves. The pool appears complete, but a mangrove tunnel, affectionately known in the area as the tunnel of love, reveals a way through to open water to the east. Then there's a hook of mangrove to paddle around before you'll see Cabbage Key less than a mile away.

Either spend the night on Cabbage Key or return directly along the east side of Cayo Costa, exploring the mangroves. Complete your circuit with a second crossing of Boca Grande Pass.

TRIP HIGHLIGHTS: The waves and sand spits of the unspoiled Cayo Costa shore and, by contrast, the green serenity of the mangrove tunnel on the east. Cabbage Key is always a gem of an experience, but Boca Grande Pass, too, can have its moments. The tidal stream can kick up a stimulating sea here with the least provocation from the wind.

TRIP RATING:

Advanced: It's the nature of the crossing of Boca Grande Pass that makes this a serious trip. What can be a rapid crossing for an advanced paddler may take a slower paddler long enough to become exposed to changing weather and sea conditions. Tides in the pass are swift.

TRIP DURATION: One or two days; 10 miles. For a two-day trip, figure on 6 miles the first day, 4 miles the second.

NAVIGATION AIDS: Large-print Waterproof Charts #25E; NOAA chart #11427.

TIDAL INFORMATION: The tide runs swiftly through Boca Grande Pass, flooding northeast and ebbing northwest. Beyond the draw of the pass, the stream is weak.

CAUTIONS: Changing weather during your trip may jeopardize your return crossing of Boca Grande Pass. Check the weather forecast and watch the weather, and be prepared to wait if conditions appear unsafe.

TRIP PLANNING: Plan ahead if you wish to stay overnight at Cabbage Key. Book a place at the inn well in advance (see this chapter's section on where to stay, for details). Midweek is best, as weekends fill with tourists. As an alternative, use the campground on Cayo Costa. Plan to begin any crossing of Boca Grande Pass shortly before slack water. The safest time is just prior to the start of the flood, so that if you have problems, the tidal stream will carry you into Charlotte Harbor rather than out into the Gulf. Refer to your tide tables.

The Mighty Tarpon

Boca Grande Pass is world renowned as one of the finest places for tarpon fishing. Flotillas of boats head for the pass when the fish are running, so if the pass is crowded when you arrive, this will be the reason. Then there's a fair chance you'll see these massive fish taking huge leaps from the water.

Tarpon is primarily an inshore fish, which grows to a large size. Although most catches are between 40 and 50 pounds, the Florida record stands at 243 pounds. That's a fair bit bigger than I am! Tarpon gulp at the surface, taking air into a rudimentary lung. This air enables them to thrive in oxygen-depleted water. In fact, tarpon are so tolerant of salinity variations that juveniles are commonly found in freshwater where there are fewer predators. A predator itself, it feeds on fish and large crustaceans. But what feeds on the tarpon?

The Boca Grande Pass and surrounding area boasts an unusually large population of hammerhead sharks, which occasionally snatch the entire body of a tarpon being landed into a boat, leaving just the head as a trophy. The Florida record for a hammerhead shark is 991 pounds, more than four times the weight of the record tarpon. This isn't meant as any kind of warning or deterrent—neither tarpon nor hammerhead are known to have a taste for kayaks.

LAUNCH SITE: Follow Route 771 southwest to Placida, or Route 775 southeast. A few hundred yards northwest of Placida, take the turn to the south, which leads to the causeway to Gasparilla Island (toll). Follow the main road until it ends at a parking area for visitors to Boca Grande Lighthouse. Drive on to get closer to the beach, where you'll see the lighthouse. It's an easy portage from here across the beach to launch into Boca Grande Pass. Note the prominent pale-blue-green gas cylinders behind you, which will provide a landmark for your return. Once you are ready to leave, move your car back to the main parking area, leaving the beachfront parking available for short-stay visitors. (There is a fee, no matter where you park.)

Cabbage Key from Boca Grande   *-79-*

DAY 1: BOCA GRANDE TO CABBAGE KEY (6 miles)

Cayo Costa lies **three-quarters of a mile**, at a bearing of 160 degrees, from Boca Grande lighthouse. The point of land you see to the right side of Cayo Costa (south) as you look across the gap is **2 miles** away (Murdoch Point). The shoreline is more interesting than the open water here, so make a straight crossing to the nearest land and then skirt the shorebreak along the beach. The big clump of pines marks the position of a campground, although the office at which you would need to register to camp lies on the opposite side of the island.

Two miles from Boca Grande, you'll reach Murdock Point. Boca Grande will become obscured by this point. At low water you may have to detour around the sandy island that extends half a mile offshore here, but otherwise float across shallows.

If you stay close to shore from here, you'll come across a clear lagoon accessible through a narrow channel (**.75 mile** past Murdoch Point). The scrub beyond the beach varies from cactus and low-growing, sand-loving plants to taller palms and trees.

By **2 miles** past Murdoch Point, you should be able to identify mangroves behind the beach. You'll then reach a place where the bleached trunks and branches of sand-worn mangroves protrude from the beach (**2.2 miles** from Murdoch Point). Pick a spot where you have an unobscured view of mangroves beyond the beach, without a fringe of sea grapes in front of you, and make a landing. Cayo Costa is very narrow here, little more than a bank of sand.

Portage across the beach to the mangrove-lined pool on the other side. Launch and paddle south (to your right) along the western beach shore until you disappear into the mangroves. A mangrove tunnel here, known as the "tunnel of love," winds through to a bay on the other side. Cross this bay to the eastern shore, just over **half a mile** from the portage, and paddle to the bay's northernmost point (**.5 mile**). Cabbage Key now lies just **half a mile** due east.

As you approach Cabbage Key, paddle around the northernmost point and follow the shore to the boat docks. Just beyond is a small sandy

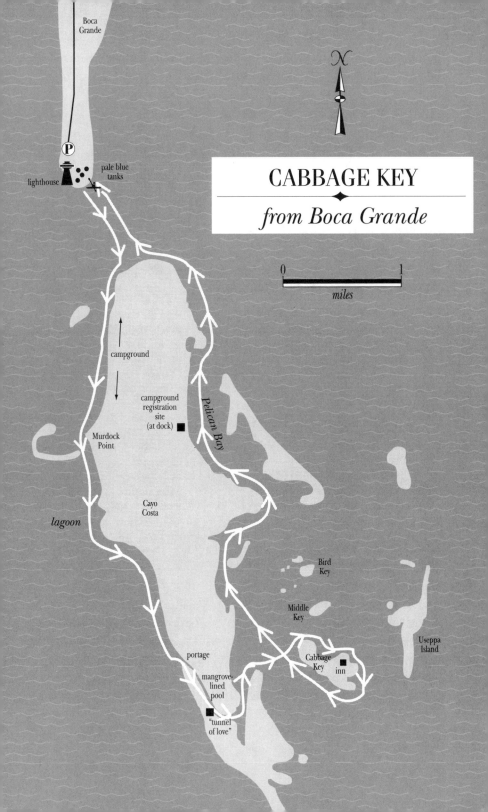

Boca
Grande

N

P

pale blue
tanks

lighthouse

CABBAGE KEY

from Boca Grande

0   1
miles

campground

campground
registration
site
(at dock)

Pelican Bay

Murdock
Point

Cayo
Costa

lagoon

Bird
Key

Middle
Key

Useppa
Island

Cabbage
Key
inn

portage

mangrove-
lined
pool

"tunnel
of love"

beach beneath coconut palms, with an old building set back in the trees. Land on the beach and pull your kayak up onto the grass. The building is Cabbage Key Inn.

DAY 2: CABBAGE KEY TO BOCA GRANDE (4 miles)

The return route from Cabbage Key to Boca Grande is shorter than the outward route. Circle Cabbage Key for **1 mile**, then head across to Cayo Costa (**.75 mile**, 310 degrees).

Explore the mangroves during your travel of less than **2 miles** to the northern tip of Cayo Costa. Be sure there are no signs of potential thunderclouds before you cross back to Boca Grande. Aim for the pale-blue gas containers.

Where to Eat & Where to Stay

LODGING and **RESTAURANT** Spend the night at *Cabbage Key Inn*. The inn is as strange as it is popular. It keeps much of the Old Florida basic wood and no frills, with bug screens, and big ceiling fans in the rooms instead of air-conditioning. This suits the colonial-style setting of the building, in the shade of luscious mature vegetation. The inn exhibits a trophy tarpon flying in front of thousands of dollar bills taped to the wall. Each dollar bears a brief message, or the name of a visitor or the visitor's loved one. It's the most impressive version of a visitor's book I've ever seen, and at a dollar an entry, the most expensive. A sign welcomes piano players, good or bad. When you look closely, you can see an old piano camouflaged there, but along with the piano stool it's festooned with leaves (dollar bills) of verdigris green. You'll also find a dimly lit and refreshingly cool bar. The restaurant here used to serve only basic fare, such as hamburgers (inspiring Jimmy Buffet's song "Cheeseburgers in Paradise." Nowadays the menu is bigger and more interesting. For information and reservations, contact Cabbage Key Inn, P.O. Box 200, Pineland FL 33945 (941–283–2278). **CAMPING** There is a campground (941–964–0375) at the northwest end of Cayo Costa. However, to use this campground, you must register at the trailer office by the dock in Pelican Bay on the east side of the island, half a mile from the camp.

Route 14:

━━ ━━ ━━ ━━ ━━ ━━ ━━ ━━ ━━ ━━ ━━ ━━ ➤

Cabbage Key from Pine Island

This round-trip to fascinating Cabbage Key with its eccentric inn takes a less committing route than the trip to Cabbage Key from Boca Grande (Route 13), with the extra safety net of possibly taking a motorboat trip back to your starting point should the weather become adverse. This trip starts on Pine Island at Mattsom Marine and follows a marked channel across the shallow waters of Pine Island Sound to the Intracoastal Waterway, and from there to Cabbage Key.

If you book accommodation at Cabbage Key Inn, you can use it as a base for venturing out to the mangrove tunnel on the east coast of Cayo Costa, and from there to stroll the Gulf beach of Cayo Costa and to explore the mangrove keys in the vicinity.

For suitably experienced paddlers, Cabbage Key makes a good starting point for a trip to circle either the southern part, the northern part, or the whole of Cayo Costa.

TRIP HIGHLIGHTS: A pleasant and straightforward paddle—but it's the destination that's the highlight. It's well worth taking the time to experience Cabbage Key Inn and Restaurant as well as the superb grounds here.

TRIP RATING:
   Basic: Using Cabbage Key as a base, additional trips around part or all of Cayo Costa may appeal to the more experienced paddler.

TRIP DURATION: The basic round trip is a full day; 10 miles. The trip can be broken into two half-day trips if you stay overnight on

Cabbage Key or Cayo Costa. Any sidetrips will add to the mileage.

NAVIGATION AIDS: Large-print Waterproof Charts #25E; NOAA chart #11427

TIDAL INFORMATION: Tidal streams are insignificant, although the water is shallow over wide areas near Pine Island, so you'll probably wish to keep to the marked route.

CAUTIONS: Be watchful for boats throughout the trip as the route follows boat channels.

TRIP PLANNING: If you plan to stay out overnight, advance booking is necessary for accommodation at Cabbage Key Inn. As an alternative, there is a campground on Cayo Costa, which adds about another mile to your paddle each way.

LAUNCH SITE: From I–75 follow Route 78 west to Pine Island. At Pine Island Center turn right (north) and after about 4 miles turn left for Mattsom Marine ($3.00 for parking, no extra charge for use of the launch ramp).

DIRECTIONS

FROM PINE ISLAND TO CABBAGE KEY: From the launch ramp, follow the marked channel that traces a route between the shallows in a direction a little north of west as far as the Intracoastal Waterway (**4.5 miles**), with its major channel markers. Cabbage Key lies directly across to the west of marker 60 of the waterway. The inn is easy to identify as the main building set slightly back from the shore. There is a small beach nearby on which to land, just short of the boat docks.

Alternatively, follow these directions from the launching ramp:

Paddle **2.25 miles** due west (90 degrees) to Part Island. Follow the coast to the northern tip of Part Island. Continue due west to Useppa Island (**1.25 miles**). Follow the coast of Useppa Island to the southern tip. Continue due west to Cabbage Key (**.4 mile**). Follow the coast north to the landing beach by Cabbage Key Inn.

FROM CABBAGE KEY TO PINE ISLAND: If you follow the buoyed channel, your return is simply the reverse of your outward journey. Otherwise, from the inn, paddle due east to Useppa Island (**.4 mile**). Then paddle to the southern tip of Useppa (**200 yards**). Cross due east to Part Island

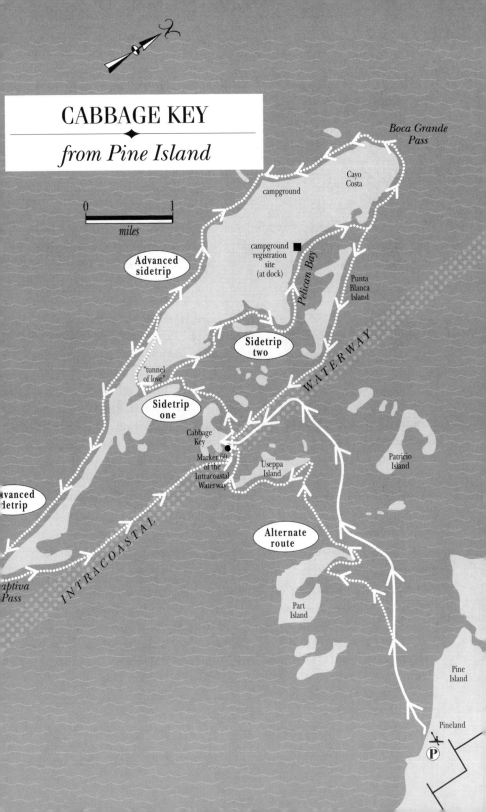

CABBAGE KEY
◆
from Pine Island

0 _____ 1
miles

Boca Grande Pass

campground

Cayo Costa

campground registration site (at dock)

Pelican Bay

Punta Blanca Island

Advanced sidetrip

"tunnel of love"

Sidetrip two

Sidetrip one

Cabbage Key

Marker 60 of the Intracoastal Waterway

Useppa Island

WATERWAY

Patricio Island

Advanced sidetrip

INTRACOASTAL

Alternate route

aptiva Pass

Part Island

Pine Island

Pineland

P

(**1.1 miles**) and follow its coast to the northern tip (**1 mile**). Paddle east to the red buoy number 10 (**.9 mile**), taking care while crossing the boat channel here. Continue east until you hit the shore of Pine Island (**.9 mile**), then paddle south to return to your launch site at Mattsom Marine (**.5 mile**).

If the weather deteriorates or you decide on a change of pace, it's possible to arrange from the inn to be ferried back with your kayak to Mattsom Marine.

SIDETRIP 1 TO THE "TUNNEL OF LOVE": A trip from Cabbage Key to the "tunnel of love" mangrove channel on Cayo Costa and a peek at the Gulf from a sandy beach will be a round trip of a little more than **2 miles**. Paddle to the northern shore of Cabbage Key, then head due west until you reach Cayo Costa. Follow the shore south until Cabbage Key disappears behind land (mangrove). Continue another **half mile** before checking the mangroves on your right for a hidden tunnel. The tunnel leads from the back of a bay.

The tunnel opens into a pool with a sandbank on your left side. Keep this sand to your left as you paddle north until you find a suitable spot for landing. There is a superb beach here, with the Gulf just a few yards away. Reverse your route to return to Cabbage Key.

SIDETRIP 2 TO OVERNIGHT ON CAYO COSTA: To camp on Cayo Costa (941–964–0375), paddle from Cabbage Key west to Cayo Costa, then follow the coast north until you see the obvious landing (about **1 mile**). You'll need to register at the office there. The campground itself is some distance away, on the northwest side of the island. Depending on the weather and likely sea conditions on the Gulf, you may wish to paddle around the shore through Boca Grande Pass to approach the campground from the beach on the west side of the island. Check at the

Cabbage Key from Pine Island

office for directions to your site. You can also reach the campground via the "tunnel of love" mangrove channel described earlier in this chapter.

SIDETRIPS FOR THE MORE EXPERIENCED PADDLER: If you've taken the "tunnel of love" route to the west side of Cayo Costa (see details earlier in this chapter), you now have a couple of interesting alternative return routes. One is to the north, with a passage through Boca Grande Pass, returning via the Intracoastal Waterway to Cabbage Key. The other is to the south, with a passage through Captiva Pass followed by a return northward along the waterway to Cabbage Key.

CAUTION: Both passes can have a strong tidal stream and locally rougher seas than elsewhere on the trip. Try to enter either pass with a rising tide to carry you through.

Where to Eat & Where to Stay

For more details on the Cabbage Key Inn, see the section on where to eat and where to stay for Route 13, Cabbage Key from Boca Grande.

Route 15:

Sanibel Island

Sanibel Island lies at the mouth of the Caloosahatchee River and offers two very different experiences to the paddler. To the north are shallow, sheltered waters with creeks extending far into mangrove forest, and to the south are exposed sand beaches. I like both, and I enjoy the contrast, so I've combined the two in this cruise that can be completed as a vigorous one-day trip for a competent paddler. However, the trip conveniently falls into two parts, each long enough to make a day trip for the less energetic. One trip explores the sand, the other the mangrove. Local restrictions prohibit overnight camping on the beach, so you'll need to arrange for a pickup if you choose the two-part option.

Sanibel's renowned Ding Darling Wildlife Refuge has protected much of the northeast-facing mangrove from development. Interpretive facilities at the refuge explain about the Florida habitats, fauna, and flora. I'd recommend a visit prior to paddling, to prepare you for what you'll see from the water. The water is shallow, with exposed mud banks and thickets of mangrove that offer perfect shelter and feeding conditions for birds such as herons and ibis.

Sanibel is also well known for its Gulf Coast beaches. The shore here is one long shell-sand beach attracting shell gatherers, who must surely carry away tons of the natural beach annually. The beach is littered with beautiful shells, small and large. The shell museum on the island can help you identify what you find.

Despite the relatively unchanging view along the sandy section of the trip, I found it both relaxing and invigorating. Shell gatherers saunter slowly along the sand, in front of low private residences that sit back from the beach among trees. In some places you'll see condominiums, with beach umbrellas and sunbathers. Flocks of wading birds drift along the shore, and pelicans and terns dive into the clear water. I watched dolphins cruise the shallows.

The lighthouse at the eastern tip of Sanibel was built in 1884 and became the focus for a small settlement into the early 1900s. The lighthouse is surrounded by trees, just a few yards from the shore.

TRIP HIGHLIGHTS: On the northeast coast, mangrove tunnels and flocks of wading birds. On the southwest shore, shell-collecting and diving birds.

TRIP RATING:
Advanced: The rating is due to its physical demands, if you do the entire 21 miles in one day. However, you can do part of the trip one day and the second part another time. Any technical difficulty can be avoided, so apart from the distance it's suitable for any paddler in suitable weather. The northeast coast has shelter, but few landings. The southwest coast is exposed to the Gulf of Mexico, but you can pull ashore just about anywhere. There are tide races (currents) in Blind Pass and off the lighthouse, but both may be avoided by portaging if you wish.

TRIP DURATION: Full day (10 hours) for the full 21 miles. If you break the trip into two parts, allow six or seven hours for each as you'll almost certainly follow a less direct route if you have more time. The part that follows the northeast shore and the mangroves is about 9 miles. The part that follows the southwest shore and the sand beaches is about 12 miles.

NAVIGATION AIDS: Waterproof Charts #25E; NOAA chart #11427.

TIDAL INFORMATION: Tidal range up to about 3 feet.

CAUTIONS: Landing possibilities are few on the mangrove section; pick a day with low chance of thunderstorms. At Blind Pass, beware of fishing lines around the bridge. Tide races form at Blind Pass and Point Ybel. There is an added hazard at Point Ybel of boats speeding close to shore.

TRIP PLANNING: Because landing is permitted in only a few places in the wildlife refuge, prepare to remain in your kayak for long periods on the northeast (mangrove) coast. Summer thunderstorms occur mostly in the afternoon, so complete the mangrove section in the morning to allow yourself the option of a quick landing on a beach in the afternoon to seek shelter. Blind Pass can be a good meeting place if you have a shore-based companion, so you can leave open your option to finish here for the day or complete a full 24-mile circuit.

LAUNCH SITE: From I–75, take exit 21 onto Daniels Parkway. Go west. Follow brown signs for Gulf Beaches. Daniels changes to Cypress Lake Drive. Turn left on Summerlin Road, which leads directly to Sanibel Island. There is a $3.00 return toll for a car to cross the causeway. Find a suitable parking spot on the causeway, by a sandy beach, and launch from there. (Parking on the island itself costs an additional 75 cents per hour.)

DIRECTIONS

FIRST PART: SANIBEL CAUSEWAY TO BLIND PASS About **9 miles**.

Paddle alongside the causeway, to Sanibel Island.

Turn right (northwest) along the shore to the power lines that cross from Pine Island (causeway to power lines, **1.5 miles**). The mouth of Tarpon Bay begins about a **quarter mile** from the power lines. Signs prohibiting Jet Skis (personal watercraft) and prohibiting access to land indicate you have reached the wildlife refuge.

SIDETRIP: Explore into Tarpon Bay, and on your left after **half a mile** you will see the entrance to a waterway extending northeast. This is the mangrove maze area described under the next trip in this guide, Tarpon Bay. Or you can continue another **mile and a half** to the back of Tarpon Bay, where there is a kayaking concession along with a cafe that serves excellent espresso. Regain the open coast by following the mangrove shore to a gap **three-quarters of a mile** to the north.

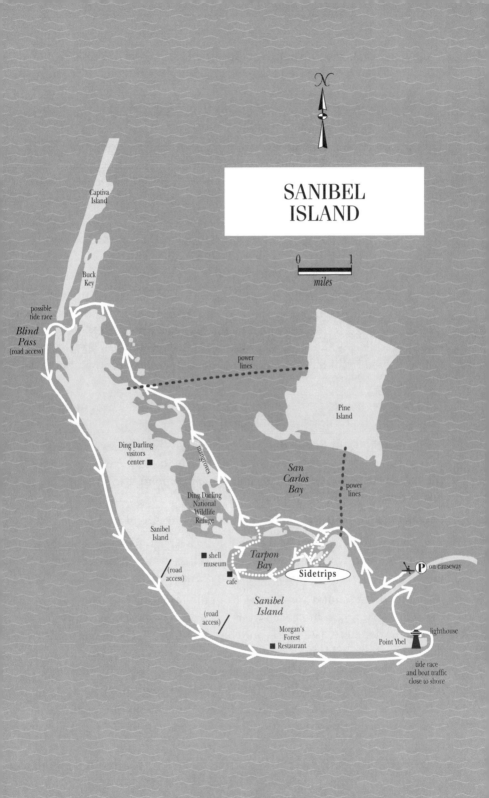

N

SANIBEL ISLAND

0   1
miles

Captiva
Island

Buck
Key

possible
tide race

*Blind
Pass*
(road access)

power
lines

Pine
Island

Ding Darling
visitors
center ■

mangroves

*San
Carlos
Bay*

Ding Darling
National
Wildlife
Refuge

power
lines

Sanibel
Island

■ shell
museum

*Tarpon
Bay*

Sidetrips

(road
access)

■
cafe

*Sanibel
Island*

on causeway

(road
access)

Morgan's
Forest
■ Restaurant

lighthouse

Point Ybel

tide race
and boat traffic
close to shore

From the entrance to Tarpon Bay, cross the narrow gap (**.25 mile**) to the mangrove islands to the west and continue your journey either on the Tarpon Bay side or on the outside of the mangrove. Another entrance to the bay appears after about **.75 mile**. If you are following the Tarpon Bay side of the mangrove islands, exit here into San Carlos Bay once more.

On the outside of the mangrove, now follow the curve of the shore (a bay) for about **.75 mile** and you will pass another gap in the mangroves. Choose between an inside route for the next couple of miles, or the outside route that follows the open shore. Refer closely to your chart if you choose the inside passage, as there are some dead ends.

You'll next encounter more power lines from Pine Island (**4.75 miles** from the first Tarpon Bay entrance). **Half a mile** beyond is a string of five small mangrove islands. Pass on either side of these islands.

At a point **1.5 miles** past the power lines, with houses to your left, enter the channel to the southwest and follow the channel markers. After **half a mile**, take the left turn indicated by the markers, which leads into a lagoon area fringed by houses on the far side, and then turn right. Follow the shore for **a quarter mile** to an exit that opens close to Blind Pass Bridge.

CAUTION: You may experience some tidal stream in the vicinity of the bridge, and also fishing lines. Portage if necessary.

You will probably notice a change in water color in the vicinity of Blind Pass as you enter the clear blue of the Gulf. The bridge marks the end of the mangrove section of the trip, and is the exit point if you wish to divide the Sanibel Island trip into two parts.

SECOND PART: BLIND PASS TO SANIBEL CAUSEWAY About **12 miles**.

The homeward journey along the Gulf shore is straightforward. Keep the land to your left. The area close to the Blind Pass Bridge displays coastal erosion, with the sea washing away the sand from beneath the trees.

At points about **5 miles** and **7 miles** from the bridge are two spots where the public can access the beach from the road. The beach may appear more crowded here. (Refer to your chart.) The beach continues to the lighthouse (nearly **11 miles** from the bridge) at the eastern end of the island. The lighthouse—a brown tube supported by a steel frame—is well camouflaged among the trees, except for the light itself.

CAUTION: A tide race develops around the point close to the lighthouse, and boats speed close to the shore here. If you are in doubt about the current, land prior to the point and check the direction and strength of the stream before either portaging around or paddling.

The causeway is around the point, **1 mile** beyond the lighthouse.

Where to Eat & Where to Stay

RESTAURANTS You'll find lots of restaurant choices on Sanibel Island. Just park and walk along until you find one that suits your taste or try *Morgan's Forest*, 1231 Middle Gulf Drive (941–472–4100), close to Sanibel Beach. It offers good food in a "tropical forest" setting. **LODGING** Sanibel Island provides numerous hotels, inns, and cottages. A central booking agency is located at 1715 Periwinkle Way (turn right at the first road junction after you get on the island). Phone (800) 726–4235. **CAMPING** The only campground on the island is at the *Periwinkle Trailer Park*, (941–472–1433) on Periwinkle Way, on the Gulf side. The charge is $22 for two people for a primitive tent site. Book at least a month in advance in winter, which is peak season. Off the island but in the area, *San Carlos RV Park* (813–466–3133) offers camping with direct access to the water close to Fort Myers Beach. Follow Summerlin Road to San Carlos Boulevard, then turn toward Fort Myers Beach. The campground will be on your left shortly before the bridge to Fort Myers Beach. *The Groves* is a quiet RV resort that also offers camping. On Summerlin Road between San Carlos Boulevard and the causeway to Sanibel Island, look for a large sign. The resort is on John Morris Road (941–466–5909).

The Mangrove Maze

When I was a young child my parents took me to Hampton
Court Palace on the outskirts of London. I can remember
the rows of chimneys on the palace roof, but it was the
maze that made the biggest impression. Dark yew hedges
squeezed over narrow dusty pathways. We children ran
backward and forward, dodging the adults until we lost our-
selves in the intricate pattern of passages and dead ends.
Benches set in the maze gave us resting places to wait and
listen beneath the gloomily oppressive walls of leaves that
towered to a height, I've found out since, of 6 feet.

Southern Florida has its own natural mazes for kayakers.
Areas of mangrove maze often measure in square miles,
with impenetrably thick walls rising up to 70 feet high. The
mangrove grows, and the maze changes. And unlike almost
all the man-made mazes of history, the floor is water.

At the end of the day at Hampton Court, an attendant on a
stepladder used to call directions to those lost in the maze.
There is no attendant to keep watch in the mangroves.
Once inside the maze, you are surrounded by tall or overhanging vegetation. The waterways turn and branch and
turn again. Many reach a dead end, but some pass through
into open pools with a choice between several possible
routes, some of which may be dead ends. It is easy to make
a mistake and get lost. When you enter a mangrove maze,
take a compass, and note where you entered in relation to
the position of the sun and the direction of any breeze. Pay
attention, and you'll probably find your way home.

Route 16:

Tarpon Bay

This route makes a circuit of Tarpon Bay, a 2-mile-long bay on the north coast of Sanibel Island. Tarpon Bay is almost completely enclosed by mangroves. The mangroves and the wildlife that lives in them are what make this area special. The water is shallow, and a string of small sand banks tufted with mangroves in the middle of the bay provide protection for birds to roost and nest, out of reach of raccoons and bobcats.

There are mangrove tunnels and mazes appear in two parts of the bay. The first of these is a way-marked route called Commodore Creek, which traces a beautiful convoluted channel through a maze of red mangrove tunnels. Be alert for wildlife. Several times I stopped paddling and allowed the current to drift me within feet of herons and egrets as they stilted across the loops of mangrove prop roots, searching for food. The way-marks ensure you can get back out easily.

At the far end of Tarpon Bay is an even greater area of mangrove maze—with no way-marks. Here I encountered vultures, egrets, and herons as I weaved my own route through the labyrinth. Mullet were leaping and splashing, adding to the sound of birdcalls and the wind through the mangrove.

TRIP HIGHLIGHTS: Mangrove tunnels and birds.

TRIP RATING:

Basic: A high level of paddling skill is not necessary if you stay out of the larger maze. The bay is shallow and almost enclosed, and

Commodore Creek offers an easy-to-follow route through a mangrove maze.

Intermediate: Map-reading skill and care is needed to explore the more distant mangrove maze that has no way-marks.

TRIP DURATION: Three hours to half a day; 6 to 10 miles.

NAVIGATION AIDS: The map issued by the wildlife refuge on payment of your launch fee is adequate for navigation here. The map is not waterproof, so take a plastic bag or map case. Otherwise use Waterproof Charts #25E and NOAA Chart #11427.

TIDAL INFORMATION: There is little tidal range, perhaps 3 feet, and insignificant current.

CAUTIONS: The access road to the launch site is gated and will be closed at the posted times. Plan to be off the water by midafternoon. This may also help avoid thunderstorms. Take a compass as a precaution if you intend to explore the mangrove maze that has no way-marks.

TRIP PLANNING: This trip can easily extend to half a day if you wish to watch the birds and explore the mangrove tunnels at a leisurely pace. Be prepared to remain in your kayak, as there are no landing areas. The water is shallow and may appear murky. Polarized sunglasses will help you see marine life more easily, and binoculars give a clearer view of the many birds.

LAUNCH SITE: Take the causeway to Sanibel Island (toll $3.00 per car for the return). Turn right at the first junction onto Periwinkle Way and follow the signs for Captiva (the next island) and after about 2.5 miles your route will lead to a cross-roads with a signpost to Tarpon Bay. At Tarpon Bay, follow the dirt road to the parking area. Pay the $3.00 launch fee at the concession building, where you can collect your map with information about the refuge.

DIRECTIONS

Turn left on launching and follow the shore about **half a mile** to the sign marking the entrance to Commodore Creek. This way-marked route links a number of the narrow waterways through the mangroves, and exits at the same point at which you entered.

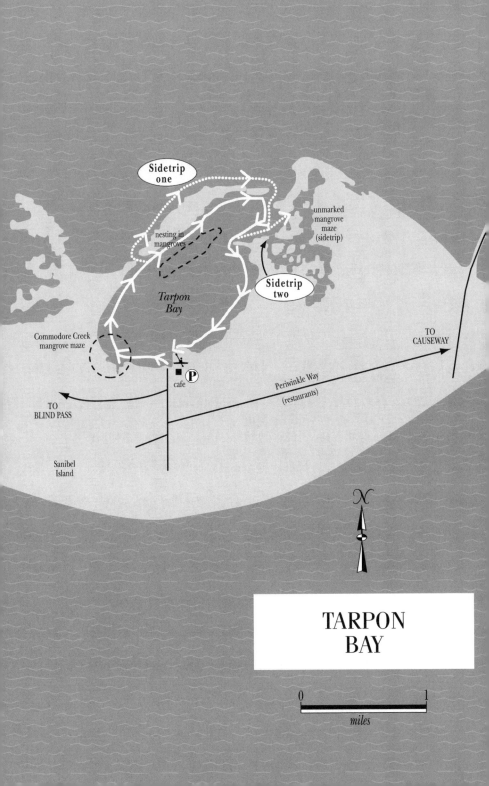

Sidetrip one

nesting in mangroves

unmarked mangrove maze (sidetrip)

Sidetrip two

Tarpon Bay

Commodore Creek mangrove maze

TO CAUSEWAY

cafe **P**

Periwinkle Way (restaurants)

TO BLIND PASS

Sanibel Island

N

TARPON BAY

0   1

miles

Continue in a clockwise direction around the northern shore of Tarpon Bay. This section ends when you have to turn south to remain in the bay, at the eastern side of an entrance (**2.5 miles** from the launch site).

SIDETRIP 1: There are several exits from the bay, the first at **1.25 miles** from the launch site. If there is sufficient depth of water, you can leave the bay to paddle up to **1.5 miles** along the northern side of the mangrove islands that enclose the bay. Any of several gaps through the mangroves will return you to the bay.

From the northeast extremity of Tarpon Bay, return in a southwesterly direction for **half a mile** to a mangrove peninsula. From this point you should be able to view the entire bay, including the launch area.

SIDETRIP 2: Head east for a quarter mile along the north side of this peninsula to the mouth of a mangrove-filled bay measuring about **1 mile** north-south and **half a mile** east-west. Many open channels, enclosed pools, narrow channels, and mangrove tunnels thread this area. But the routes are unmarked, and you'll need to rely on your compass and sense of adventure to explore here.

Follow the Tarpon Bay coast southwest for **1.25 miles** to return to the launch site.

Mangroves in Color

Florida displays only three types of mangrove (red, white, and black), but their differences involve more than simply color.

The red is easiest to identify by its arching, branching, and looping prop roots—sometimes so smooth and rodlike, and of such a copper red, that they could be a plumber's nightmare in copper pipe. Rods also extend straight down from branches to the water, mud, or sand below. Typically these props branch handlike into a number of fingers that appear to grasp the beach below as if attempting to lift a handful of sand or mud. The prop roots contain surface cells that provide the roots with oxygen. Although the plant grows in salty water, the roots are able to reject salt, leaving the sap with the salinity typical of other plants.

The white mangrove often sends out prop roots to form an above-ground cone spreading out from the trunk, but the roots don't exhibit the flamboyant arching or the copper color of a red mangrove. The tree sometimes sends up woody, fingerlike spikes that stick out of the mud, allowing buried roots to breath in waterlogged soils. On beaches, these spikes (called pneumatophores) catch through holes in seashells, making it look as though someone has spent hours collecting shells with holes in them and then threading them over the spikes. For positive identification of the white mangrove, look at the leaf: it's elliptical.

The black mangrove commonly has many pneumatophores that are fleshy rather than woody and about pencil-size, extending 6 inches or more above saturated soil. They grow longer when the average water depth is greater. The black mangrove has lance-shaped leaves, yellow-green on top and gray-green underneath.

Mangroves form dense thickets that colonize shallow water and banks of mud or sand. The prop roots and pneumatophores trap drifting debris and also provide a spot for oysters and sponges to grow on. Eventually sufficient material collects to turn the mangrove thicket into a low island. The process eventually slowly progresses to the point where other species of tree are able to colonize.

Where to Eat & Where to Stay

RESTAURANTS A cafe in the concession building at Tarpon Bay serves excellent espresso. The concession staff can recommend a place to eat among the wide variety of restaurants on Sanibel. **LODGING**   Numerous hotels, inns, and cottages are on the island. A central booking agency is located at 1715 Periwinkle Way. (You will pass it on your way across the island after making your first right turn.) Phone (800) 726–4235. **CAMPING**   The only campground on the island is at *Periwinkle Trailer Park* on Periwinkle Way, on the Gulf side (941–472–1433). Off the island but in the area, *San Carlos RV Park* (813–466–3133) offers direct access to the water close to Fort Myers Beach. Follow Summerlin Road to San Carlos Boulevard, then turn toward Fort Myers Beach. The campground will be on your left shortly before the bridge to Fort Myers Beach. The *Groves* is a quiet RV resort offering camping. On Summerlin Road between San Carlos Boulevard and the causeway to Sanibel Island, you will see a large sign. The resort is situated on John Morris Road (941–466–5909).

Route 17:

■ ■ ■ ■ ■ ■ ■ ■ ■ ■ ■ ■ ■ ■ ■ ■ ■ ■ ➤

Matlacha Pass

This is a cruise among the keys of the Matlacha Pass National Wildlife Refuge, starting from Punta Rassa boat ramp near Fort Meyers. The keys, in shallow water west of Punta Rassa, offer ideal natural shelter and food for wading birds. The keys are mostly signed as no-landing areas as part of the wildlife refuge. The tall condo building close by the ramp makes a perfect landmark for your return.

TRIP HIGHLIGHTS: Bird-watching in shallow water.

TRIP RATING:
Basic: However, exposed in windy weather.

TRIP DURATION: 3 hours; 5.5 miles. Sidetrip: add 1 hour and about 2 miles.

NAVIGATION AIDS: Large-print Waterproof Charts #25E; NOAA chart #11427.

TRIP PLANNING: Tidal range is small, but it can be an advantage to paddle around high tide because of very shallow water.

LAUNCH SITE: Follow State Road 867 from Fort Meyers toward the toll booth before the Sanibel Causeway. For the Punta Rassa boat ramp, turn right at the last exit just before the booth. The ramp is signed to your left, where a short one-way road leads to the ramp for unloading and onward to the parking area and restrooms. Parking is $3.00 per day.

The fish-cutting tables on the docks by the ramp attract pelicans and herons, making this a good place to observe and photograph these birds at unusually close range.

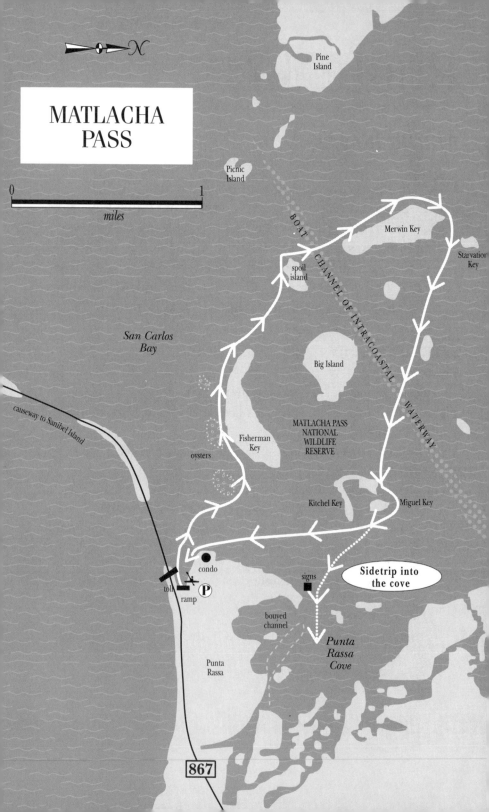

MATLACHA PASS

N

0   1

miles

Pine
Island

Picnic
Island

Merwin Key

Starvation
Key

spoil
island

*San Carlos
Bay*

Big Island

MATLACHA PASS
NATIONAL
WILDLIFE
RESERVE

Fisherman
Key

oysters

causeway to Sanibel Island

Kitchel Key

Miguel Key

condo

**Sidetrip into
the cove**

toll

ramp

signs

P

bouyed
channel

*Punta
Rassa
Cove*

Punta
Rassa

867

Follow the shore to your left on launching from the ramp until you reach open water. The causeway stretches across to Sanibel Island to your left, with the southern tip of Pine Island just to the north of west. Pine Island will be partially obscured by the group of keys making up part of the Matlacha Pass National Wildlife Refuge.

Cross to Fisherman Key, **three-quarters of a mile** to the northwest, avoiding the oyster beds close to the key.

Continue to the northwestern tip of the key, then cross to the spoil island **half a mile** to the northwest. (A spoil island is an area of sea where dredged material is dumped, thus forming an island.)

From the northwestern side of the spoil island, cross for a **quarter mile** to Merwin Key.

CAUTION: A boat channel crosses your path halfway across the gap between the spoil island and Merwin Key. Watch for boats, and don't linger.

Follow the coast of Merwin Key to its northern point. From here set off on a course of approximately 100 degrees, which will take you past two spoil islands to Miguel and Kitchel Keys. These keys partly encircle an area of shallow water that dries as mudflats at low tide—a great spot for bird-watching. (The sidetrip to Punta Rassa Cove, described below, begins here.)

From here, use the prominent landmarks to guide you the final **1.2 miles**. Paddle south toward the Sanibel Causeway and use the condo development as a position marker. Hug the shore from the condos onward, and you will be guided back to the launch ramp.

English Knees and Water Depth

This morning I was pouting like a parrot fish and repeating the address "Boothe Bird Museum, Brighton." Now the expert of the institution, Mr. Adams, is viewing me with a puzzled expression. "What were you wanting, again?" he gently encourages.

"We spoke on the phone last week. I'd like to measure heron's legs."

"Heron's legs! Hmmm. Let's see! We have a heron upstairs. Why did you want to measure . . . herons' legs?"

"Actually, I wanted to be able to judge the depth of water from a distance."

"Common Grey Heron. Of course you won't be able to tell the depth exactly; it'll depend on how the heron's standing." He's got a point there. He opens a door and I pass a stuffed zebra head as I mount the stairs behind him. There are more pieces of large mammal. Is that a buffalo? In a bird museum? But here's a heron! It seems tiny as I crouch down and open my father's tape measure to the spindly leg. Six inches from foot to knee, and another six inches above the knee, although the thigh runs into feathers.

"Actually I'm sea kayaking in Southern Florida. There's a lot of shallow water there. It would be useful to gauge the depth by observing herons standing in the water."

"Ah!" He pauses. "You've got different species there. The great blue's bigger of course, but you can estimate proportionately."

I'm only after a rule of thumb. Every clue is helpful. Where you see a mid-sized heron, or an egret, or a white ibis, with water to its knees, (6 inches), there's enough depth to make slow progress in a kayak. The knees of the taller (4 foot) great blue heron, standing straight, indicate 9 inches.

SIDETRIP: Punta Rassa Cove extends **1 mile** east of the northern point of Punta Rassa. Paddle southeast from Kitchel Key to the prominent signs that stand at the entrance to the cove. Wherever you explore within this key-studded bay, find your way out by paddling west and looking for the channel markers that lead across the southern part of the cove to the exit. On leaving the cove, follow the shore south past the condos to the launch ramp. A visit to the cove will add about **2 miles** to your trip.

Where to Eat & Where to Stay

RESTAURANTS   To reach ***Channel Mark***, at 19001 San Carlos Boulevard in Fort Myers Beach (941–463–9127), drive east on Summerlin Road to San Carlos Road (south). Cross the first bridge to find Channel Mark or continue to the second bridge to find the ***Bridge*** restaurant on your left at 708 Fisherman's Wharf (941–765–0050). The Bridge is waterfront, and like Channel Mark, offers a good menu with variety. **LODGINGS**   This area is rich with accommodations, so call visitors information in Sanibel (941–472–1080), Fort Myers (941–332–3624), or Fort Myers Beach (941–454–7500). **CAMPING**   *San Carlos RV Park* in Fort Myers Beach has camping (941–466–3133).

Route 18:

■■ ■■ ■■ ■■ ■■ ■■ ■■ ■■ ■■ ■■ ■■ ➔

Orange River

S potting and identifying a manatee for the first time can be a tricky process. Someone will call out "Manatee!" and all you'll see is ripples in widening rings. This trip offers a unique opportunity to view manatees in the warm outflow water from a power plant. Here you'll be able to note their above-water appearance so you'll know what to look for, so you can recognize manatees when you see them from your kayak.

The Orange River is a tributary of the Caloosahatchee River, entering the Caloosahatchee close to the I–75 bridge and near a power plant. The river stained my white kayak orange, so maybe it's the color of the water in the river that led to its name.

The Orange River runs through quiet rural development, with houses both old and new bordering one or both banks for most of its length. With the waterfront as an attraction, most houses present a harmonious profile when viewed from the water, even if the level of development prohibits landing at any point. Some of the houses are old, and the gardens mature. In particular there seems to be a wide variety of bromeliads and tree ferns in the trees along the river, many obviously introduced into the gardens, but others most likely escaped and apparently faring well.

Upstream from the launch site the river becomes progressively overgrown to the point where vegetation creates a tunnel around the river. Downstream, the river runs into mangrove, where manatee-watching tour boats drift, and anglers cast.

This is not a dramatic trip, but if you're prepared to look around and watch for manatees, then a journey upstream as far as the river permits, and then downstream to the wildlife refuge on the Caloosahatchee at the point of its confluence with the Orange, should offer a really pleasant day. Combine it with the magic of watching manatees in the warm water of the power station outflow, floating and surfacing and rolling just a few yards from the observation walkways, and you could have a perfect day.

TRIP HIGHLIGHTS: Watching the manatees. Upstream, bromeliads and the foliage in general. Downstream; the rookeries and roosting islands in the Caloosahatchee River.

TRIP RATING:
Basic: Straightforward paddling.

TRIP DURATION: Upstream round-trip: half-day; up to 7.5 miles, depending how far upstream you manage to get. The fuller the

Manatees

According to the Manatee Information Center on the Orange River, about one in every thirty-six manatees in the United States is killed each year from human-related causes, mostly from boat collisions. An estimated 1,800 manatees are in U.S. waters.

Manatees swim south in winter, so that's when you're most likely to see them in Southern Florida. Manatees love the warm-water outflow from power plants such as the one by the Orange River and elsewhere in Florida.

Look for a broad tan back without dorsal fin, a snout with two nostrils, or a round tail flipper like a giant version of a sea grape leaf.

Manatees generally surface to breathe every three or four minutes. Patience, and timing with a watch, can help your success rate in spotting a manatee resurfacing, as can some estimation of the speed and direction of travel. Manatees often swim along at a similar pace to kayaks, surfacing at intervals within easy sight, but frequently a sighting may consist of a hurried movement to get out of the way of the boat.

The Mote Marine Laboratory and Aquarium on Lido Key, near Sarasota, features a massive tank holding manatees.

river, the farther upstream you may be able to get if there are no fallen trees blocking the route, but the current will be stronger. Downstream round-trip: 1.5 hours; 3 miles.

NAVIGATION AIDS: USGS topographic 1:24,000 maps "Fort Myers" and "Olga."

TIDAL INFORMATION: Upstream the current will always be flowing back toward your starting point. Downstream you'll end up returning against the current.

TRIP PLANNING: The gate at Lee County Manatee Park opens and closes automatically, opening at 8:00 A.M. and closing in winter (October through March) at 5:00 P.M. The manatees are frequently seen through much of the winter. They are seldom seen in summer, when the water elsewhere is warm enough for them to travel in comfort. Check the manatee viewing update line (941–694–3537). Carry a drink bottle and snacks in your kayak, as no landing is permitted on the Orange River except at Manatee Park.

LAUNCH SITE: The Lee County Manatee Park is located on State Road 80, 1.5 miles east of I–75 exit 25. There is a parking fee of 75 cents per hour, maximum $3.00 per day, but no launch fee. Launching is from a tiny dock into a narrow creek that runs into the Orange River. The power plant is about .5 miles away, across State Road 80.

DIRECTIONS

Launch from the ramp and follow the narrow passage to the Orange River. When you reach the river, look around to familiarize yourself with the landmarks you will watch for on your return.

UPSTREAM ROUND-TRIP: Turn left from the launching creek and continue just as far as you wish, or can. You will pass beneath two sets of power cables, and after about an hour you should come to a quiet road bridge (**3 miles** from the launch site).

The river forks a **quarter mile** beyond this bridge. Take the left fork. There is a second road bridge shortly after, and it is unlikely you will be able to continue much higher up the river from this point because of

Orange River

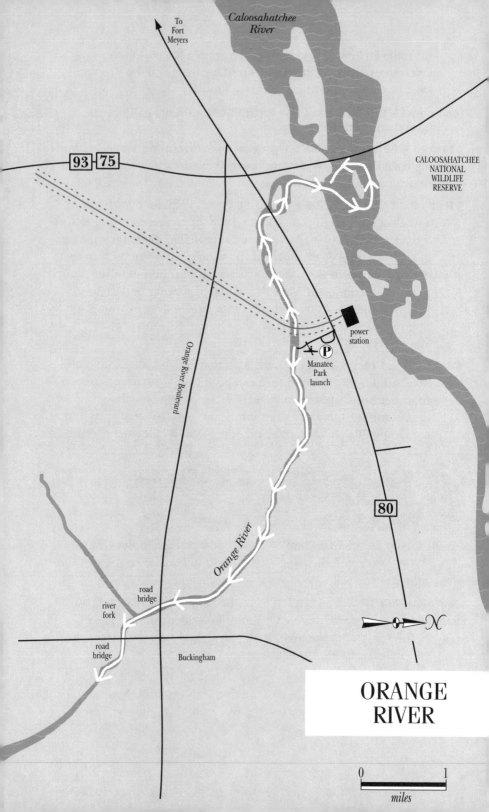

To Fort
Meyers

*Caloosahatchee
River*

93 75

CALOOSAHATCHEE
NATIONAL
WILDLIFE
RESERVE

power
station

P

Manatee
Park
launch

Orange River Boulevard

80

Orange River

road
bridge

river
fork

road
bridge

Buckingham

N

ORANGE
RIVER

0   1
miles

insufficient water or fallen trees blocking the way. At any point in the ascent, you can turn around and cruise back down.

DOWNSTREAM ROUND-TRIP: From the launching creek in Manatee Park, turn right on reaching the Orange River. After a short distance the banks become obscured with mangroves, and islands appear in the waterway. **A mile** below the park, you will pass under the concrete bridge carrying State Road 80. A **quarter mile** farther is a pool with docks and derelict boat sheds. Turn right here. The confluence with the Caloosa-hatchee is now just another **quarter mile** downstream.

You will see the big, white outline of two manatees mounted as a memorial by a mangrove island in the Caloosahatchee. The island is a busy nesting and roosting site for birds. Upstream is the power plant, with its tall chimneys, and downstream is the massive I–75 road bridge.

Despite the noise, this area really is a designated National Wildlife Refuge, and you should see a lot of birds here. Paddle around and look at the natural Florida vegetation, embellished with a few exotics and escapees. Paddle beneath the roaring turnpike that stretches mangrove-like across the river on its concrete tap roots. Then return up the Orange to Manatee Park to have a last look at the peaceful manatees in the outflow of the power plant.

Where to Eat & Where to Stay

RESTAURANTS No local recommendations. **LODGING** The best bet is to seek accommodations in the Fort Myers area, which is within day-trip driving distance of the Orange River. **CAMPING** *San Carlos RV Park* (813–466–3133) permits camping and offers direct access to the water close to Fort Myers Beach. Follow Summerlin Road to San Carlos Boulevard, then turn toward Fort Myers Beach. The campground will be on your left shortly before the bridge to Fort Myers Beach. *The Groves*, a quiet RV resort, also has camping. Watch on Summerlin Road between San Carlos Boulevard and the causeway to Sanibel Island for a large sign to The Groves, which is situated on John Morris Road (941–466–5909).

Route 19:

Mound Key

Mound Key in Estero Bay is the site of large Indian shell mounds, dating to 1400 B.C. The main village of the Calusa tribe was positioned here, and the 125-acre site is protected by the state as a historical landmark. The northern mound is about 28 feet high; the southern one is 40 feet high, one of the tallest in Florida. A canal that once joined the two mounds is now little more than a marshy area.

Some of the largest gumbo limbo trees to be found are on Mound Key—some as tall as 50 feet, and 10 feet around.

TRIP HIGHLIGHTS: Easy trip to a historic site dating back more than three thousand years.

TRIP RATING:
   Basic: Straightforward paddling.

TRIP DURATION: 2 to 2.5 hours; 5 miles.

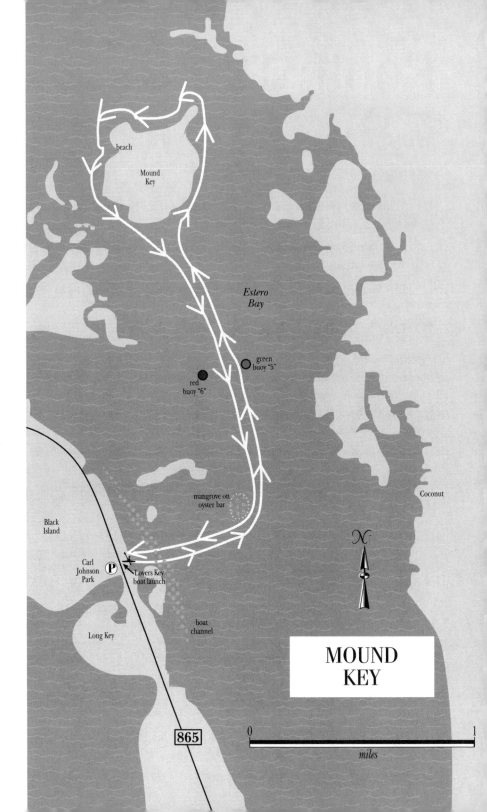

beach

Mound
Key

*Estero
Bay*

green
buoy "5"

red
buoy "6"

Coconut

mangrove on
oyster bar

N

Black
Island

Carl
Johnson
Park

Ⓟ

Lovers Key
boat launch

boat
channel

Long Key

MOUND
KEY

0   1

miles

865

NAVIGATION AIDS: Waterproof Charts #25E (inset C); NOAA chart #11426.

TIDAL INFORMATION: Range 4 to 5 feet.

LAUNCH SITE: From I–75 exit 18, head west on Bonita Beach Road (865) for 9 miles. Carl Johnson Park will be on your left, and Lovers Key boat launch will be on your right.

DIRECTIONS

From Lovers Key boat launch, paddle **half a mile**, at 60 degrees, across the main boat channel to a small oyster bar with a red mangrove growing on it.

The largest island visible slightly west of north from this oyster bar is Mound Key. Paddle **1.4 miles**, at 15 degrees, to reach Mound Key. On the way, you'll pass close to buoys marking a half-mile-wide boat channel, which you will cross.

Follow the island shore in a counterclockwise direction until, after about **1 mile**, you reach a small inlet. Enter the inlet and beach your kayak here to hike the trail to the top of Mound Key. Along the trail you'll find historical interpretive signs.

From the inlet, continue around the coast for **half a mile** to the southern shore. Retrace your path for **2 miles** to the launching place.

Where to Eat & Where to Stay

RESTAURANT See page 105 for suggestions in Fort Myers, located about 8 miles north on Route 865. **LODGING** See listings on page 105. **CAMPING** Koreshan State Park (941–992–0311), 9 miles north of Bonita Beach Road on U.S. 41 (Tamiami Trail), has tent and camper sites.

Route 20:

Black Island

This trip threads through protected waterways in a barrier island area in Estero Bay, with the option of venturing onto the Gulf Coast beach. The west-facing Gulf beach is a good vantage point for watching the sunset.

The route circles the Lovers Key State Recreation Area. Call for information on the area and its wildlife (941–463–4588).

TRIP HIGHLIGHTS: Sheltered trip with good chance of seeing wildlife.

TRIP RATING:
   Basic: A short and easy route.

TRIP DURATION: 2.5 to 3 hours; 5 miles. Sidetrip: add 1 hour and about 1.5 miles.

NAVIGATION AIDS: Large-print Waterproof Charts #25E; NOAA chart #11426.

TIDAL INFORMATION: Range 4 to 5 feet.

LAUNCH SITE: From I–75 exit 18, head west on Bonita Beach Road for 9 miles. Carl Johnson Park will be on your left, and Lovers Key boat launch will be on your right.

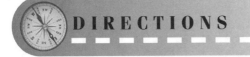

DIRECTIONS

From Lovers Key launch, head south (to your right) and follow the channel markers for **1 mile** to green marker 29. Turn right under the bridge north of Big Hickory Island (**.2 mile**).

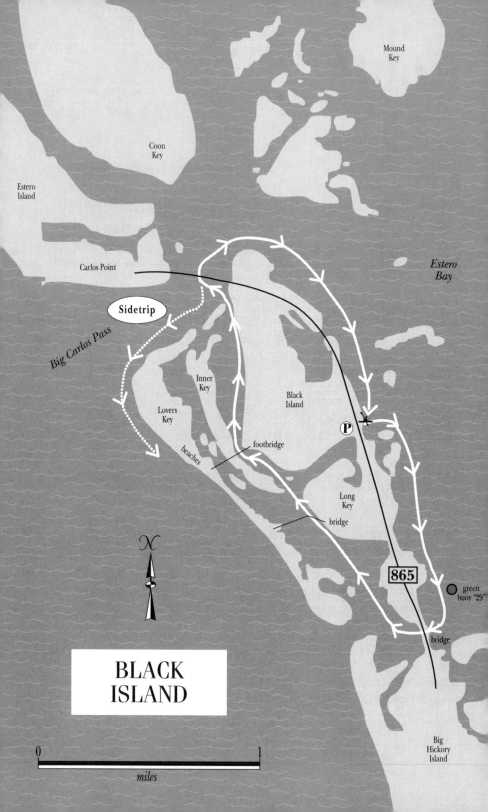

Mound
Key

Coon
Key

Estero
Island

Estero
Bay

Carlos Point

Sidetrip

Big Carlos Pass

Inner
Key

Black
Island

Lovers
Key

P

footbridge

beaches

Long
Key

bridge

N

green
buoy "29"

865

bridge

BLACK
ISLAND

Big
Hickory
Island

0   1

miles

Now keep to the right shore (shallow water in places) and head north-west and north for about **1 mile**.

You'll now reach a bridge that crosses from Lovers Key to Long Key, with a bridge support on a tiny island. You can go under the bridge on either side of this tiny island, but then return to the Long Key shore on your right.

The shore continues northwest for about **200 yards** before it curves around to the north-east.

Leave the shore at this point and continue northwest into the mouth of a channel ahead (Black Island will now be on your right, Inner Key to your left) until the channel narrows to pass beneath a footbridge (**.3 mile**). (There are restrooms close to the bridge, on Black Island.)

Follow the channel as it widens to the north and head for Carlos Point Bridge. The deeper water is to the right, close to Black Island. It is **three-quarters of a mile** from the narrows to the Carlos Point Bridge.

The Gumbo Limbo

It's easy to identify a gumbo limbo tree by its shiny, peeling, reddish bark—although when the tree has good soil and plenty of water, it grows faster and has a more silvery bark.

The gumbo limbo is a salt-tolerant tree, although it doesn't grow in saltwater, like the red mangrove. Its trunk expands with stored water in the rainy season and shrinks during the dry season.

The wood from gumbo limbo trees, marketed as West Indian birch, is a traditional material for voodoo drums. Resin from injured bark was prized by pre-Columbian Mayas as a varnish for canoes and as incense.

Once under the bridge, follow the shore of Black Island for **1.3 miles** to return to your launching point.

SIDETRIP: From Carlos Point bridge, paddle southwest out through Big Carlos Pass to find some beautiful beaches on Lovers Key—a good place for watching the sunset. Add **a mile and a half** or so for this sidetrip to the beach. *Caution:* You may experience rough conditions in the pass, especially on a falling tide.

Where to Eat & Where to Stay

For information on lodging, camping, and restaurants, see the section on where to eat and where to stay for Route 19, Mound Key.

Route 21:

----- ----- ----- ---- ---- --- --- --- -- -- ➤

Wiggins Pass

Here is an easy, enjoyable paddle through mangroves and along the beach. Development has spoiled some of the natural look of the area, but it still offers some beautiful paddling.

The beaches on the Gulf face west here and often provide good surfing conditions—"the best in the Naples area," according to Chris Siegfried of Naples Sea Kayaking Adventures. Look for Chris playing in the waves aboard his kayak if there's a good storm!

The west-facing beach also makes a perfect grandstand for viewing the sunset. The direct return route from the entrance to Wiggins Pass is less than 1 mile, so you can watch the sunset and still have time to make an easy return to the launch site before dark. Or during a full moon, return by moonlight.

TRIP HIGHLIGHTS: Good sunset trip; if you enjoy surf, pick stormy weather for waves.

TRIP RATING:
   Basic: A sheltered trip in windy weather.

TRIP DURATION: 2 hours; 3 miles.

NAVIGATION AIDS: Waterproof Charts #25; NOAA chart #11430.

TIDAL INFORMATION: Tidal range 4 to 5 feet.

CAUTIONS: Heed cautions for Florida as a whole.

TRIP PLANNING: Take bug screen if you plan to watch the sunset on a still evening.

LAUNCH SITE: Follow I–75 to exit 17, then head west on Route 846 (Immokalee Road) 3.5 miles to U.S. 41 (Tamiami Trail). Turn right and go 1.5 miles to County Road 888 (Wiggins Pass Road). Turn left. After 1 mile, turn left at County Road 901 (Vanderbilt Drive) and drive just 100 yards; on your right is Cocohatchee Park, with a boat ramp (no launch fee if you are not using a trailer).

DIRECTIONS

Keep to the left shore after leaving the launch ramp and as you go around two corners and to the bridge ahead. At the bridge cross to the right shore and go around the point hugging the shore. Pass the entrance to one small channel (don't go under the road here) and enter the next narrow waterway. This waterway will lead you to another road bridge with shallows consisting of oyster beds. Be careful of your hull!

Keep right when you reach Water Turkey Bay. You'll find the entrance to Vanderbilt Channel here, which will lead you to Wiggins Pass, by which point you will have paddled about **2 miles**. Keep left through the Pass to reach the sea.

CAUTION: The current can be swift in the channel. Keep to the side for slower water. You may find surf on the Gulf, so approach the final entrance with caution, and if in doubt, land early to check the conditions.

THE RETURN JOURNEY: Follow the channel markers for a little more than **half a mile** to the condominiums and the launching ramp.

Where to Eat & Where to Stay

RESTAURANTS The *Emmond's Tia Cafe* in the Green Tree Plaza in North Naples at the corner of Route 846 (Immokalee Road) and Route 31 (Airport Road) comes highly recommended. **LODGING** Try *Fairways Resort* at 103 Palm River Boulevard, Naples, FL 34110, off Immokalee Road (Route 846) west, 3 miles from I–75 (941–597–8181). **CAMPING** *Koreshan State Historic Site* in Estero, 10 miles north of this trip on U.S. 41, offers camping (941–992–0311).

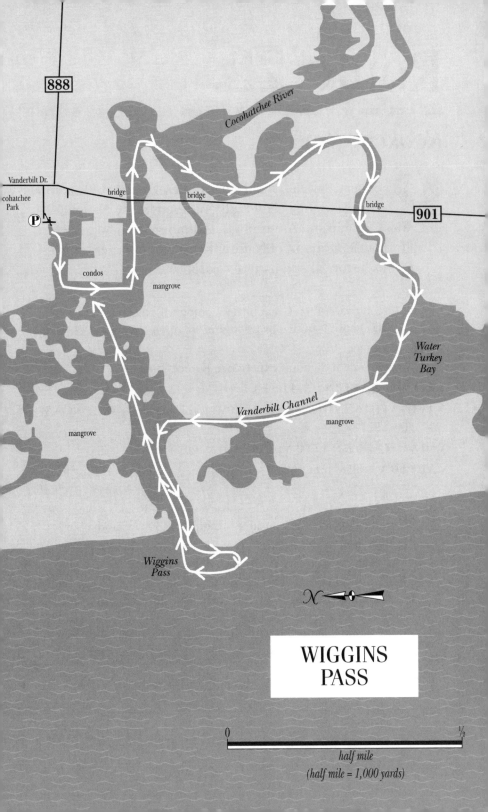

888

Cocohatchee River

Vanderbilt Dr.
cohatchee Park
bridge   bridge   bridge   901
P

condos

mangrove

Water
Turkey
Bay

mangrove

Vanderbilt Channel

mangrove

Wiggins
Pass

N

WIGGINS PASS

0   ½

half mile
(half mile = 1,000 yards)

Route 22:

▬ ▬ ▬ ▬ ▬ ▬ ▬ ▬ ▬ ▬ ▬ ▬ ➤

Rookery Bay

Rookery Bay National Estuaries Reserve is a 9,400-acre environmental center administered by the National Oceanic and Atmospheric Administration and the Florida Department of Natural Resources in order to protect its historical and natural treasures.

TRIP HIGHLIGHTS: Great bird-watching with a combination of narrow channels in mangrove and more open bay.

TRIP RATING:
Basic: Some navigation experience is necessary.

TRIP DURATION: 3–4 hours; 5.5 miles

NAVIGATION AIDS: Large-print Waterproof Charts #41E; NOAA chart #11430.

TIDAL INFORMATION: Tidal range 4 to 5 feet.

CAUTIONS: Pay attention to your route as there is opportunity to stray.

TRIP PLANNING: Bird-watching is excellent in Rookery Bay, especially in late spring, so consider bringing binoculars and a bird identification book.

LAUNCH SITE: Rookery Bay is located between Naples and Marco Island. From I–75 exit 15, head south on State Route 951. After 7 miles you'll cross U.S. 41 (Tamiami Trail). Continue south on Route 951 for a further 2.5 miles, where you should see a sign for Briggs Nature Center on your right, at the turn on to Shell Island Road. Turn right and drive 2 miles to the end of the road, your launch site.

DIRECTIONS

From Shell Island Road, paddle north. Keep left of the small mangrove island and look for an opening with an orange channel/trail marker with a white sign. Follow trail markers through small bays and canopied mangrove channels (a wandering 280 degrees). When you exit the mangrove tunnel you will be entering Rookery Bay.

Here you leave the trail markers. Paddle west into the bay, then head north to the entrance to Stopper Creek.

Stopper Creek winds sharply for a little more than the first **quarter mile** before branching. Keep left at this junction.

From here the creek widens gradually, and any tidal stream will slacken. Follow the creek for almost **1.5 miles** to the next junction.

Turn left into Lager Bay and head west for **.2 miles**. You should then be able to see two small mangrove islands to your left and an opening to your right. Pass through the opening and then head west again. This will bring you to another gap, this time leading to First National Bay (watch out for shallow water here).

Approximately west of here are two mangrove islands; head for them. When you reach the second one, turn left and head south. From here the opening into Rookery Bay will be evident.

Bird Haven

Rookery Bay is full of islands small and large and is home to many species of bird. In late spring the mangrove islands provide a haven for thousands of hatchlings, presenting an excellent opportunity for bird-watching.

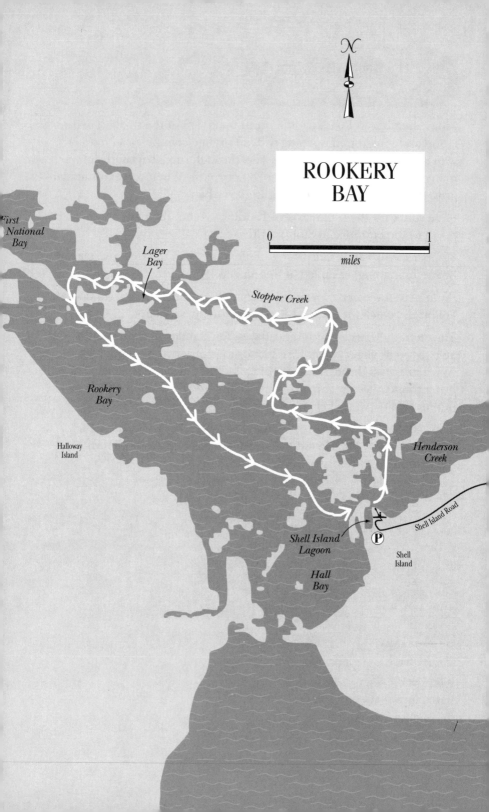

ROOKERY BAY

First National Bay

Lager Bay

Stopper Creek

0 ⸻ 1
miles

Rookery Bay

Halloway Island

Henderson Creek

Shell Island Road

Shell Island Lagoon

P

Shell Island

Hall Bay

Head southeast through Rookery Bay toward Hall Bay (**1.5 miles**, 130 degrees). A string of mangrove islands separates Rookery Bay from Hall Bay.

Once in Hall Bay, follow the main channel markers to Henderson Creek (southeast, then northeast). You'll pass a tall stone monument on your right. Your starting point is **65 yards** further on to your right.

Where to Eat & Where to Stay

RESTAURANTS Try the family-owned *Pelican Bend Restaurant* on the Isle of Capri, 1 mile north of Marco Island. **LODGINGS** *Comfort Inn and Suites*, just off I–75 exit 15 (941–353–9500). See the Kice Island/Cape Romano trip (Route 24) for additional accommodations. **CAMPING** You'll find primitive camping sites on U.S. 41 (Tamiami Trail), east toward Miami as you cross the Everglades, but the closest is about 18 miles from the Shell Island Road launching site. See Route 24 for additional camping facilities.

Route 23:

Halloway Island

This trip makes a circuit of Halloway Island, passing through Rookery Bay. The many mangrove islands in Rookery Bay provide nesting sites for thousands of birds. Late spring is a good time to be here to watch the hatchlings, but avoid disturbing the birds.

TRIP HIGHLIGHTS: Great bird-watching in Rookery Bay; some narrow channels with good paddling.

TRIP RATING:
Basic: Some navigation experience is necessary.

TRIP DURATION: 3 to 4 hours; 5 miles.

NAVIGATION AIDS: Large-print Waterproof Charts #41E; NOAA chart #11430.

TIDAL INFORMATION: Range of 4 to 5 feet.

TRIP PLANNING: Binoculars and a bird identification book can heighten the enjoyment of bird-watching.

LAUNCH SITE: Rookery Bay is located between Naples and Marco Island. From I–75 exit 15, head south on State Route 951 for 9.5 miles to Shell Island Road (look for the brown Briggs Nature Center sign). Turn right into Shell Island Road and drive 2 miles to the road end, your launch site.

DIRECTIONS

From Shell Island Road, head north for **.25 mile**. Keep left of the small mangrove island and look for an opening with an orange channel/trail marker with a white sign. Follow the trail markers through small bays and canopied mangrove channels (a wandering 280 degrees). When you

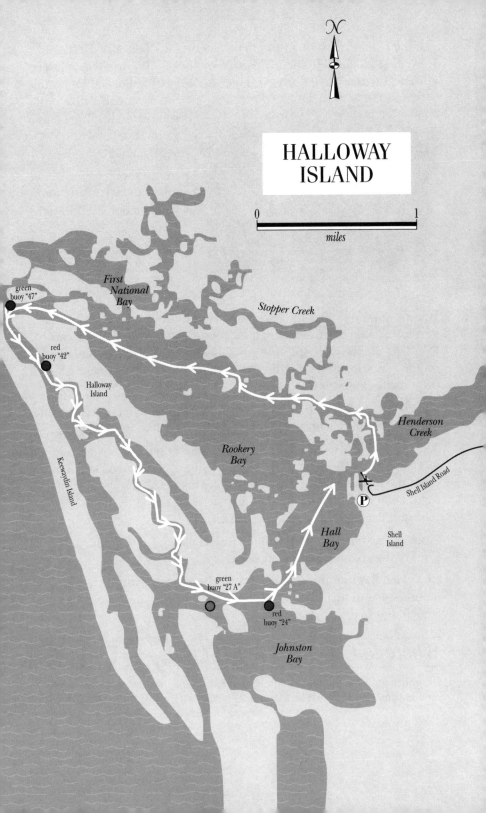

exit the mangrove tunnel you will be entering Rookery Bay. Here you leave the trail markers and paddle across Rookery Bay to the northwest corner (**1.5 miles**, 290 degrees). Enter Rookery Channel and follow this

waterway **half a mile** until you reach the green navigation marker 47.

Turn left into the Intracoastal Waterway and follow the left (east) shore to a junction beyond red marker 42.

Turn left and follow the channel, keeping Halloway Island on your left. When you meet the Intracoastal Waterway again, follow the Halloway Island shore (on your left) into a narrow bay that extends almost a mile southeast into Halloway Island. Don't go all the way to the end; you'll need to paddle about **half a mile** until you reach an inlet on the right. Follow the small channel that leads from the back of this inlet.

CAUTION: The next section is tricky to follow at high tide, with false trails that lead nowhere, and is also tricky at extremely low water levels.

The channel leads for about **half a mile** before branching. Turn left but follow the right shore until you reach the Intracoastal Waterway, as indicated by channel markers. Green channel marker 27A will be on your right. Follow the channel markers east across the northern end of Johnston Bay until the reach red marker 24.

From red marker 24 turn northeast into Hall Bay. Look out for shoals in front of the channel on the left side.

Cross Hall Bay into the channel beside Shell Island. Pass the tall stone monument and turn right at the point to return to your original launching place.

Where to Eat & Where to Stay

For information on lodging, camping, and restaurants, see the section on where to eat and where to stay for Route 22, Rookery Bay.

Route 24:

▬▬ ▬▬ ▬▬ ▬▬ ▬▬ ▬▬ ▬▬ ▬▬ ▬▬ ▬▬ ▬▬ ▬▬ ➤

Kice Island and Cape Romano

Cape Romano Island and adjacent Kice Island are barrier islands just south of Marco Island. The trip details two outings: one around Kice Island, and the other beyond Kice Island to Cape Romano. Both begin and end at Caxambas Pass Marina.

The western shores have long white beaches with solitude and seashells. Excellent camping places are available on Morgan Bay at Cape Romano, along the shores of Kice Island, and at the western end of Blind Pass, so both of these outings may be taken as a day trip or stretched across a couple of days. Local paddler Chris Seigfried detailed these routes for me.

TRIP HIGHLIGHTS: Sheltered waterways behind beautiful barrier-island beaches.

TRIP RATING:
Basic: Some navigation experience is necessary; this trip requires even more experience if the Gulf of Mexico is rough.

TRIP DURATION: Kice Island: about 3 hours; 7 miles. Cape Romano: 4.5 to 5 hours; 10 miles. Add to this to make beach explorations. Either route will make a good full-day trip or can be spread over two days with an overnight camp.

NAVIGATION AIDS: Large-print Waterproof Charts #41E; NOAA chart #11430.

TIDAL INFORMATION: Be watchful for signs of water running out from passes into the sea, as this may cause choppy conditions locally. Paddling through Morgan River can be difficult at low tide due to shallows (Cape Romano trip).

CAUTIONS: The Gulf coastline is exposed to wave action. Be sure to check the weather forecast before leaving. As an extra precaution you can drive to the west coast of Marco Island to look at the conditions before you go. As a safe alternative to paddling back along the Gulf coast in rough weather, consider simply reversing your outward route.

TRIP PLANNING: The launch site opens at dawn and closes at dusk, with no overnight parking permitted. Be sure to return before dusk. However, there are great camping areas all along both Kice Island and Cape Romano, so if you can arrange to be dropped off at the launch site and picked up the next day, you can choose any one of many spots along the beach to spend the night.

LAUNCH SITE: From exit 15 off I–75 travel 7 miles south on State Road 951 to Marco Island. Once over the bridge to Marco Island, travel 4.5 miles farther on 951 to Caxambas Pass Marina, which is nearly at the end of the road, on the right. You can't miss it! Launching is free to kayakers if you don't have a trailer.

DIRECTIONS

KICE ISLAND (7 miles)

This getaway offers wilderness camping, good fishing, beautiful beaches, and the west coast contrast between open beaches and tight mangrove channels.

Head south for **half a mile** from Caxambas Pass Marina to Dickmans Island. You can paddle either between Dickmans Island and Currys Island or between Dickmans Island and Dickmans Point. Either way, resume your southerly course as soon as you are clear of Dickmans Island until you reach the shore of Kice Island, then turn southeast.

About **1.35 miles** from the marina, you'll reach the entrance to Grassy Bay. In the southeast corner of Grassy Bay, about **half a mile** from the entrance, is a narrow creek that will lead you to more open water at Snook Hole Channel.

Turn right and continue southeast for **three-quarters of a mile** to Blind Pass. Enter this pass to the right and follow it for **1 mile**. Here is a great camping spot with some good fishing in the pass.

Kice Island and Cape Romano

xambas Pass

Dickmans
Point

Dickmans
Island

Currys
Island

Fred Key

Grassy
Bay

Snook Hole
Channel

Helen
Key

Kice
Island

Blind Pass

Morgan
River

Morgan
Bay

Cape Romano
Island

Cape
Romano

Morgan
Pass

Morgan
Point

N

KICE ISLAND
◆
AND CAPE ROMANO

0   1

miles

At the Gulf end of the pass, turn right and head north along the white beach for **2 miles** until you reach Dickmans Point. Turn east to enter Caxambas Pass.

For the next **half mile**, cross to Dickmans Island and follow the north shore until the marina becomes visible again from behind the unnamed island to the north of Dickmans Island. Then paddle **half a mile** back to the marina via the tip of the unnamed island.

CAPE ROMANO (10 miles)

This route extends the range of the Kice Island trip to Cape Romano. The outward route is through sheltered channels, and the homeward route is along open coast. But if conditions appear unsuitable on the Gulf, you can remain in sheltered water.

Follow the same route as for the first part of the Kice Island trip from Caxambas Pass Marina—through Grassy Bay and the creek to Snook Hole Channel and southeast to the entrance of Blind Pass (**3 miles**).

Instead of turning right, into Blind Pass, paddle a **quarter mile** south across the pass to the western side of a small bay. Enter the bay, which narrows into the Morgan River and follow the river to Morgan Bay (**1.2 miles**).

CAUTION: Paddling can be difficult in Morgan River due to shallows.

To the west and southwest of here across Morgan Bay are good beaches for camping. Note the remains of homes that failed to withstand the encroachment of the Gulf of Mexico.

Cross Morgan Bay to the entrance to Morgan Pass, paddling southwest for **half a mile**. Paddle through Morgan Pass to the Gulf at Morgan Point on Cape Romano (southeast, **.7 mile**).

To return to the marina, paddle back northwest along the Gulf shore to Blind Pass (**1.75 miles**). From here follow the beach to Dickmans Point (**2 miles**).

Cross from Dickmans Point to the northwest tip of the unnamed island lying to the north of Dickmans Island (**.4 mile**, 55 degrees) and continue on the same bearing to your starting point (**.3 mile**).

Kice Island and Cape Romano

Where to Eat & Where to Stay

RESTAURANTS   Snacks and beverages are available at *Caxambas Pass Marina*. Kayaker Chris Siegfried recommends the grouper sandwich at *Pelican Bend restaurant*, at 219 Capri Boulevard, on the Isle of Capri, a mile north of Marco Island (941–394–3452). **LODGING**   There is accommodation available close to I–75 at exit 15, such as *Comfort Inn and Executive Suites*, 3860 Tollgate Boulevard, Naples FL 34114 (941–353–9500). Closer to the launch site, near the junction of U.S. 41 and Route 951, is the *East Trail Motel*, 11381 East Tamiami Road, Naples, FL 34413 (941–774–2165), e-mail:johnirwin@printmail.com. **CAMPING**   Take your pick of good wild camping spots on the beaches of *Kice Island* and *Cape Romano Island*, but no overnight parking at Caxambas Marina. *Get Wet Sports* on Isle of Capri, 203 Capri Boulevard, Naples FL 34113, will provide a shuttle so you can leave your car elsewhere. Additional camping is available at *Naples/Marco Kamp of America*, 1700 Barefoot Williams Road, Naples FL 34113 (941–774–5455). There are also primitive camping sites adjacent to U.S. 41 as you cross the Everglades and head toward Miami. The closest is about 18 miles away, with signs posted on U.S. 41.

Route 25:

━━ ━━ ━━ ━━ ━━ ━━ ━━ ━━ ━━ ━━ ━━ ━━ ➤

Fakahatchee Island

Fakahatchee Island is rich with cultural history, including remnants of a Calusa Indian mound, about 20 feet tall, dating back for more than two thousand years. You will also see reminders of the European settlers who hunted, trapped, farmed, and made moonshine here. There are the ruins of two homes and a graveyard that date back more than a century.

TRIP HIGHLIGHTS: A pleasant trip to an island with a lot of history.

TRIP RATING:
Intermediate

TRIP DURATION: 4.5 to 5 hours; 12 to 14 miles.

NAVIGATION AIDS: NOAA chart #11430.

TIDAL INFORMATION: Tidal range of 4 to 5 feet.

CAUTIONS: Take care with your navigation if you explore the myriad islands generally south of your route.

LAUNCH SITE: From I–75 exit 15, head south on County Road 951 to U.S. 41 (Tamiami Trail). Head east for 14 miles to Port of the Islands marina (to your right). Turn right at the main entrance, and after 60 yards turn left to the marina. There is a $3.00 launch fee per kayak.

Farewell

By Michael Gray

A few years ago I paddled out among the mangroves to bid farewell and give thanks to the keys of Southern Florida for another season's enjoyable experiences. I had just finished several weeks of guiding paddlers down mangrove-lined channels and along shell beaches. This environment had grown dear to me, and now I needed to spend a little time alone in it.

I was enjoying the pepper-scented breezes swirling around the mangroves when I saw a dolphin feeding along the root line at the edge of the channel. Suddenly it broke from its feeding and sped toward my boat, pushing a strong wake off its domed forehead. My alarm turned to glee as this swift mammalian cousin of mine turned on its side, inches from my boat, to look directly up at me. As I peered into one bright gleaming eye, I knew that someone, not something, knew exactly why I was here.

DIRECTIONS

From the boat launch, head south down Faka Union Canal and River for **3 miles** to Faka Union Bay. The canal offers straight, easy paddling.

From red marker 50, paddle into the large opening in the mangroves that lies at 150 degrees, about **half a mile** away. This channel will narrow in about a **quarter of a mile** and then open into Fakahatchee Bay.

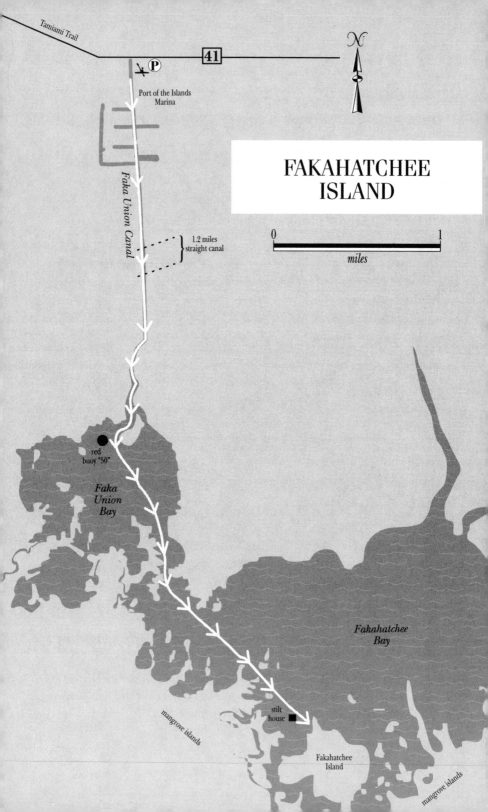

Tamiami Trail

41

Port of the Islands
Marina

Faka Union Canal

1.2 miles
straight canal

N

FAKAHATCHEE
ISLAND

0   1

miles

red
buoy "50"

*Faka
Union
Bay*

*Fakahatchee
Bay*

mangrove islands

stilt
house

Fakahatchee
Island

mangrove islands

From the narrows you should be able to see the ruins of a stilt house on a bearing of about 140 degrees and **1.2 miles** away. This stilt house is close to the northern tip of Fakahatchee Island. Cross to the ruin, passing it to the left (north) to land on the oyster shell beach beyond.

Explore the island on land, or paddle around the island, (a distance of about **2 miles**. As you paddle around the island, keep to the shoreline until you see the house ruin once more, using it to orient yourself before heading back across the Bay.

To return to your starting point at the marina, retrace your path to Faka Union Bay (320 degrees) and follow the eastern shore of the bay to the mouth of the Faka Union River and Canal.

Where to Eat & Where to Stay

RESTAURANTS *Port of the Islands marina* has a restaurant and bar (813–394–3101 or 800–237–4173). Also try *the Oyster House* in Everglades City, across from the Everglades Park headquarters, next to Glades Haven Campground. **LODGING** *The Port of the Islands Hotel* near the launch site offers accommodations (813–394–3101 or 800–237–4173). **CAMPING** Camping is permitted without permit on *Fakahatchee Island* because it lies outside Everglades National Park, though it's a bad spot for biting flies unless the weather is cold and blustery. There are some primitive camp sites along U.S. 41; watch for the signs as you drive east. In Everglades City, east on 41, about 14 miles from Port of the Islands, you'll find *Glades Haven RV and Campground* (941–695–2746).

Route 26:

▬ ▬ ▬ ▬ ▬ ▬ ▬ ▬ ▬ ▬ ▬ ▬ ▬ ➤

Everglades City Circuit

You'll find a little of each of the main ingredients of the Everglades coast within this one five-day journey. Starting and finishing at Everglades City, the trip begins by traversing a region of mangrove keys to reach the outer coast with its shelly shorelines and sand spits, where you can watch the sun set into the sea.

After looping south on this outer fringe, you leave behind the open horizon and run deep into the Everglades until you reach brackish water and finally float onto clear fresh-water right at the border of the Everglade Prairie, with its giant lake of saw grass. (Unfortunately you are unlikely to see much of the saw grass, which lies hidden behind the taller waterfront fringe of mangrove that lines even the tightest creeks.)

Your return to Everglades City follows the northern section of the Wilderness Waterway, leading through open lakes and narrow twisting channels. The full Wilderness Waterway links Everglades City to Flamingo, about 99 miles to the south, so you are more likely to see a little more boat traffic on this final part of the route.

TRIP HIGHLIGHTS: Variety of Everglades wilderness experiences, during a multiday tour. This is your opportunity to experience the magic of camping out for a number of nights on sand beaches, chickees, and land sites within Everglades National Park.

The Watson Mystery

Watson's Place is on the highest point of land in the area, site of a massive Calusa Indian shell mound. An exploration of the mound reveals signs of the man known as Ed Watson—house foundations and remains of the vats in which Watson boiled down sugar cane.

The story of Ed Watson is a strange one. In the late nineteenth century, Watson was imprisoned in Arkansas for stealing horses. Later, a warrant was issued for his arrest in connection with the murder of the outlaw Bella Starr, but he skipped the area and headed for the Everglades, a place mostly out of reach of the law.

Watson bought forty acres of Calusa Indian shell mound from the widow of Will Raymond, killed in a shootout while resisting arrest. Watson grew sugar cane and rendered it down in large iron vats to make syrup, which he sold in Tampa and Key West. But rumors about how he dealt with his workers—mostly men with no family ties who supposedly disappeared after working for a time with Watson—came to a head when the weighted-down bodies of three of them were discovered by clam diggers.

Watson laid the blame on one of his workers, a man named Cox. The sheriff was reluctant to visit the old shell mound to investigate, and Watson offered to arrest Cox and bring him back. But when Watson next returned to Chokoloskee, he carried Cox's hat—a bullet hole through it—and said he had shot Cox. Most of the villagers present when Watson offered his story were suspicious of him, and said so. Watson is said to have aimed his shotgun at the crowd and fired.

Someone shot at Watson, then most of the crowd opened fire. Watson died. No single person could be identified as the killer, and there was not a full investigation.

The Watson mystery caught the imagination of Peter Matthiessen, who wrote the 1990 novel *Killing Mister Watson* about the case.

TRIP RATING:

> *Advanced:* The trip is committing and physically demanding. Although conditions may turn out to be benign, the multiday nature of the trip makes it better suited for the experienced paddler.

TRIP DURATION: 5 days; 45 miles.

DAY 1: Everglades City to Rabbit Key; 12.6 miles.

DAY 2: Rabbit Key to Mormon Key; 7.4 miles.

DAY 3: Mormon Key to Sweetwater Chickee; 7.4 miles.

DAY 4: Sweetwater Chickee to Lopez River; 10 miles.

DAY 5: Lopez River to Everglades City; 7.4 miles.

> If you wish to add an additional night at any one of the camping places, this should be planned with the Park Service at the time of registration for this trip within Everglades National Park.

NAVIGATION AIDS: Waterproof Charts #41; NOAA chart #11430. The park center at Everglades City has charts and maps for sale.

TIDAL INFORMATION: The tidal range exceeds 4 feet in some locations. In general, rising tides flood inland from the Gulf and falling tides drain outward to the Gulf. The ebb, or falling, tide tends to be slightly stronger than the flood owing to the fresh water that drains from the Everglades swamps, and the stream generally dissipates when it reaches the open water of the Gulf.

CAUTIONS: The tidal streams can be swift in some of the channels, so plan to travel with the tide.

TRIP PLANNING: Because of the ferocity of bugs in summer, October through March is the best period to travel. This is also the season of lowest thunderstorm activity. Check the weather forecast when you register, for you may wish to modify your plans accordingly. Find out at the park center whether landing is currently permitted on Indian Key.

LAUNCH SITE: From I–75 take exit 14A. Drive south on Route 29 for 21 miles to Everglades City. Follow the main road through town, as if continuing to Chokoloskee. Everglades National Park headquarters is signed to the right. There is free parking in the vicinity of the park center, where you will register for any multiday trip and purchase a backcountry camping permit ($10 per trip for up to six people). Launching to the north side of the park building is free. Alternative launching sites are alongside the causeway between Everglades City and Chokoloskee.

DIRECTIONS

DAY 1: EVERGLADES CITY TO RABBIT KEY (12.6 miles)

Depart toward Indian Key Pass (**1 mile** away, at a true bearing of 250 degrees). You may be able to see the small beach that lies south of the entrance to this marked pass, or observe powerboats entering or leaving the channel. (Alternatively, paddle **half a mile** northwest along the shore from the park center launch site, then follow the channel markers that cross Chokoloskee Bay in a southwest direction for **1 mile** from Barron River to the entrance of Indian Key Pass.)

From here, Indian Key is **3.75 miles**. Simply follow the channel markers through Indian Key Pass.

CAUTIONS: The falling tide runs swiftly from Chokoloskee Bay toward the Gulf. Leave yourself plenty of room in order to avoid the upstream ends of the spoil islands (islands created by heaping up material from channel dredging) that expose coral rock and a tangle of mangrove.

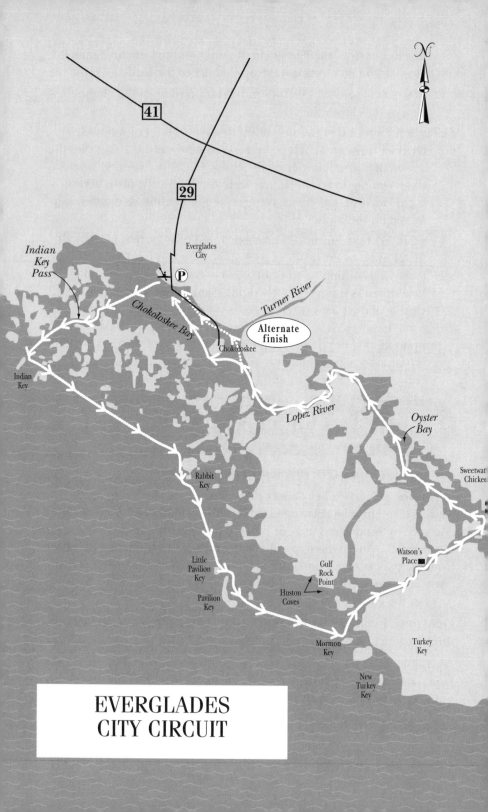

EVERGLADES CITY CIRCUIT

Powerboats generally keep to the deeper water of the buoyed channel, so watch for traffic before crossing the channel to cut corners. As the pass opens, Indian Key lies straight ahead (225 degrees), with sand beaches.

From the southwest point of Indian Key, Rabbit Key is visible. You can now take the direct route to Rabbit Key (**5.75 miles**, at 125 degrees), or follow the alternative route described in the following paragraphs. A sand spit forms northeast from Rabbit Key at low tide. Paddle around the spit or approach from the south of the island to find a campsite close to the east of the spit. There's a toilet facility on the beach. Although you will need to skirt the island to watch the sunset, the rising sun in the morning will drive away the bugs.

A more interesting, alternative route from the northern tip of Indian Key skips from key to key until reaching Rabbit Key. Following are step-by-step details for this route, with mileage and compass bearings.

INDIAN KEY TO KINGSTON KEY (**.6 mile**, 125 degrees).

KINGSTON KEY TO COMER KEY (**1.7 miles**, 125 degrees). Landing is permitted on Comer Key.

COMER KEY TO JEWEL KEY (**5 mile**, 105 degrees). Follow the shore to the eastern tip (**.3 mile**).

JEWEL KEY TO DEMIJOHN KEY (**1 mile**, 110 degrees). There is a small mangrove key almost halfway to Demijohn.

DEMIJOHN KEY TO TURTLE KEY (**1 mile**, 135 degrees).

TURTLE KEY TO LUMBER KEY (**5 mile**, 120 degrees).

LUMBER KEY TO RABBIT KEY (**1.2 miles**).

Follow the coast of Lumber Key clockwise to the southeastern point (**.4 mile**), then cut across to the mangrove point on an unnamed key (**.4 mile**, 235 degrees). From here the landing on Rabbit Key is close across the gap (**.4 mile**, 270 degrees). A sand spit dries between the mangrove island and Rabbit Key. At low tide the approach from this side offers the shortest beach portage. The primitive toilet facility is here.

DAY 2: RABBIT KEY TO MORMON KEY (**7.4 miles**)

Paddle from Rabbit Key to Little Pavilion Key (**2.1 miles**, 155 degrees), then on to Pavilion Key (**.8 mile**, 155 degrees). Pavilion Key lies roughly halfway between Rabbit and Mormon Keys. Easy landings on sandy beaches make Pavilion Key a good lunch spot.

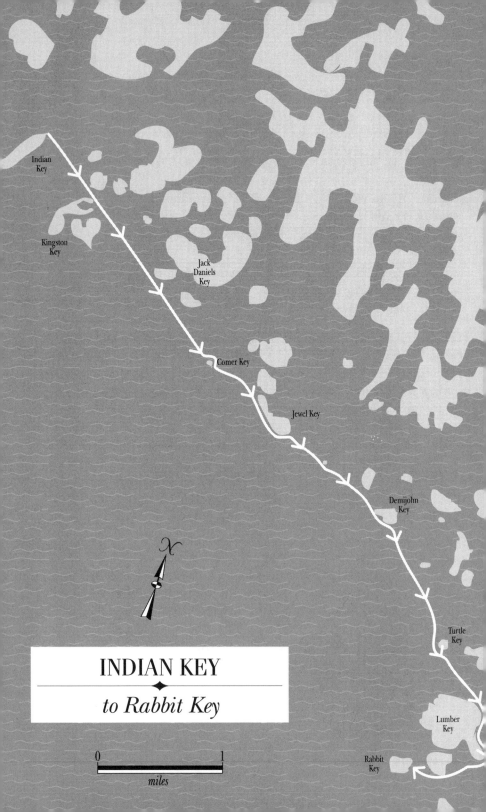

Indian Key

Kingston
Key

Jack
Daniels
Key

Comer Key

Jewel Key

Demijohn
Key

Turtle
Key

INDIAN KEY

◆

to Rabbit Key

Lumber
Key

Rabbit
Key

0   1

miles

Rabbit Key

It was dark. We sat beside a small fire sipping dark French-roast coffee beneath a brilliantly starry new-moon sky. From behind us, in the mangroves, came a loud crunching and scrabbling sound. Raccoons, we supposed. Scott shone a flashlight in their direction and a pair of orange eyes glowed back. I stood up and strolled along the shore toward the mangrove on the point. I never reached the raccoons.

The rising tide had overflowed into a small creek feeding the mangroves inside the sand beach that circles the island. Water was rushing in, dark and noisily. There in the stream were glowing balls of light; greenish lights that bounced and swirled in the fast current, finally weaving among the mangrove roots to disappear out of sight. I was spellbound.

I switched on my flashlight, aiming it at one of the glowing objects speeding past, and was perplexed to see nothing there. I switched off the light and the glow reappeared. I laughed, bemused. Then one ball of light caught in the shallow inside of a bend and I tried again, directing a beam of light onto it. Now I could see what was causing the glow.

It was a transparent jellyfish, the size of a plum. When jostled in the current, ridges of light flashed on in a citrus-segment pattern. These glowed for a number of seconds before fading, until another collision sparked them into light again. Scott and I stood and marveled at the sight, until the mosquitoes drove us back to the smoke of the fire.

The direct route from Pavilion Key to Mormon Key involves paddling to the southern tip of Pavilion Key (about **1 mile**), then crossing open water to Mormon Key (**2.75 miles**, 110 degrees).

A more interesting route to Mormon from Pavilion is to island-hop. From the northern tip of Pavilion, paddle **1 mile** east to a gap in the keys. Continue east until you hit the mangrove shoreline **1 mile** beyond. To the southeast is Gulf Rock Point (**1 mile**), with the two Huston Coves setting in to your left. Follow the coves to Gulf Rock Point, then cross to

Mormon Key (**1.4 miles**, 150 degrees). The obvious beach landings with good camping are on the north shore.

You can extend your day by exploring Turkey and New Turkey Keys, on which landing is permitted, and the adjacent islands. A tour to round both Turkey Keys will total **5 miles**.

DAY 3: MORMON KEY TO SWEETWATER CHICKEE (7.4 miles)

Depart on a rising tide. The Chatham River opens **1 mile** (bearing 25 degrees) from Mormon Key. The entrance is disguised by a number of mangrove islands. Follow the strongest tidal flow up the river until you are clear of the islands (about **1 mile** northwest). At this point, you will see water leading to the left and right, and the Chatham River curves to the right.

A further **2 miles** upstream is Watson's Place, on the left side of the river. This is your only landing possibility before Sweetwater Chickee. There is a camp site here.

From Watson's Place, continue upstream, taking the right-hand branch at the first fork in the river (**.4 mile**). **Three-quarters of a mile** farther is another fork. Follow the right-hand channel for less than **half a mile** until you hit marker 99 of the Wilderness Waterway.

From here continue for about **three-quarters of a mile** at about 60 degrees until you reach a junction. At this point, the entrance to the creek leading to Sweetwater Chickee is about **300 yards** away on a bearing of 20 degrees.

Follow Sweetwater Creek upstream to Sweetwater Chickee. The chickee stands hidden from your approach by an island with a few palm trees in among mangroves.

Take a detour before landing to explore the freshwater creek upstream for the few yards possible until it becomes too entangled by overgrowing mangrove to progress farther. Look for the impressive bromeliads in this area.

DAY 4: SWEETWATER CHICKEE TO LOPEZ RIVER (10 miles)

Paddle downstream to the mouth of Sweetwater Creek (**1 mile**). Your view will now be largely obscured by islands with channels vanishing between them. Paddle northerly for about **half a mile**, at 310 degrees, until you see the expanse of Last Huston Bay extending ahead.

Cross Last Huston Bay to marker 103 of the Wilderness Waterway (**1.2 miles**, 300 degrees). The markers are arrow-shaped, nailed to posts,

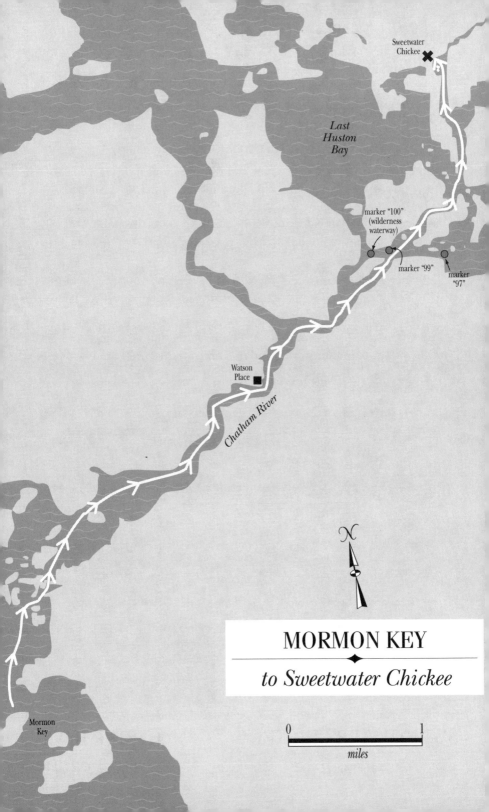

Sweetwater
Chickee

Last
Huston
Bay

marker "100"
(wilderness
waterway)

marker "99"

marker
"97"

Watson
Place

Chatham River

N

MORMON KEY

◆

to Sweetwater Chickee

Mormon
Key

0   1

miles

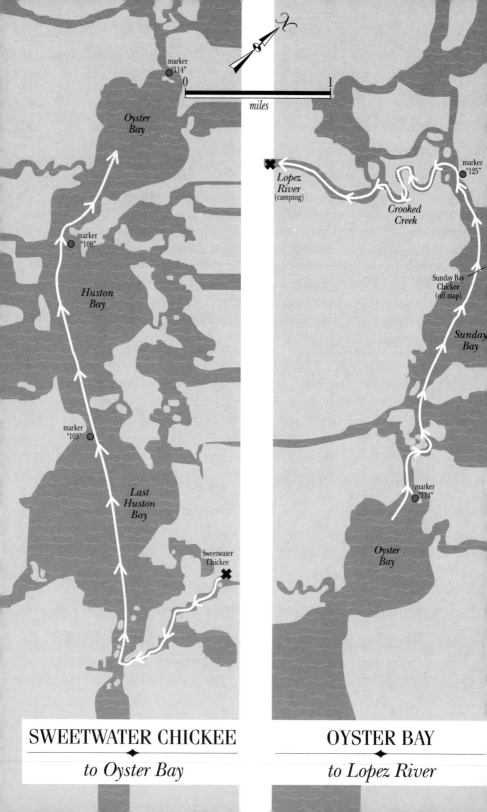

marker "114"

Oyster Bay

0

1

miles

marker "108"

Huston Bay

marker "103"

Last Huston Bay

Sweetwater Chickee

Lopez River (camping)

marker "125"

Crooked Creek

Sunday Bay Chickee (off map)

Sunday Bay

marker "114"

Oyster Bay

SWEETWATER CHICKEE
◆
to Oyster Bay

OYSTER BAY
◆
to Lopez River

often crowned with a live royal tern (but be aware that neither the terns nor the arrows indicate the direction to follow).

From marker 103, follow the marked route across Huston Bay (or take a direct route, bearing about 300 degrees) to a choke of islands and shallows beginning at marker 108.

A small bay follows the choke, and this ends in another group of islands.

Beyond the islands lies Oyster Bay.

Cross Oyster Bay to the northwest exit at marker 114 (**1 mile**, 310 degrees). (Markers are placed for navigational convenience and are numbered from Flamingo upwards to Everglades City.) The route now weaves through narrow waterways for **three-quarters of a mile**, in a generally northwest direction, to Sunday Bay. The marker posts are closer together and well positioned on this stretch.

Sunday Bay has a chickee, should you be in need of a place to land. Parallel the southwest shore of Sunday Bay for **1 mile** (330 degrees) until you see the opening on your left.

CAUTION: Pay attention to your navigation on this next section, from Sunday Bay to Lopez River. The convoluted path of the waterway, together with the appearance of junctions, can easily lead you astray.

From Sunday Bay, enter the waterway (290 degrees) and continue for **half a mile** until marker 125, showing the entrance to Crooked Creek (entrance directly to the southwest).

Crooked Creek snakes down to the Lopez River. At marker 126 (almost **1 mile**), your route hairpins back to the left. Keep to the left shore if in doubt.

Lopez River descends generally southwest. The Lopez River campsite is on your left just before a sharp right bend in the river. (**.8 mile** beyond marker 126). This is a land site, not a chickee, but it is easy to spot.

DAY 5: LOPEZ RIVER TO EVERGLADES CITY (7.4 miles)
From the Lopez River campsite, the route becomes straighter and widens. Follow the right shore for **2 miles**, by which point Chokoloskee will be in sight, and you will spot houses. When the southern tip of the island becomes visible, cut straight across the bay toward it (**1.2 miles**, 305 degrees).

Paddle northwest along the southern Chokoloskee shore. You'll pass the Smallwood Store Museum (no landing unless you are visiting the museum) and some small marinas to the westernmost point, from which you'll see Everglades City. Now either cut across the bay (**2 miles**, 330 degrees) and follow the shore for the last few yards, or paddle the shoreline around the bay (**2.75 miles**) to return to your original launch site at Everglades City.

You also have the choice of an alternative route from the Lopez River campsite to Everglades City. From the mouth of the Lopez River, follow the right-hand shore to the mouth of Turner River (**3.5 miles**). Cross the river mouth in a northwesterly direction for **three-quarters of a mile** and continue into the channel beside the road causeway. Follow the causeway for **half a mile** until you reach the bridge. Pass under the bridge and follow the bay shore for the final **half mile** back to the park canoe ramp at Everglades City. This alternative is preferable if the wind is against you, and is actually shorter by **three-quarters of a mile** than the Chokoloskee route.

Where to Eat & Where to Stay

RESTAURANTS   The *Rod and Gun Lodge* (P.O. Box 190, Everglades City, FL 34139; 941–695–2101), which is situated across the street from The Bank (see Lodging below) serves dinner from 5:00 till 9:00 P.M. Anticipate a step back in time into the dim, cool atmosphere of a hunting and fishing clubhouse, with its trophy alligator hides and bobcat skins, stuffed fish, and historic photographs of magnificent catches. Ask about the current catch on special before selecting your meal. As a contrast, *J.T.'s Island Grill* in Chokoloskee is a lighthearted store and grill with tables inside and also out on the deck. Expect paper plates and a plastic tablecloth, but a cheerful and chatty atmosphere. J.T.'s is signposted on the right of the road just past Chokoloskee Post Office as you drive through town. **LODGING** The bed and breakfast known as *The Bank* is located in the imposing old Bank of Everglades building, 201 West Broadway, in the center of town. The Bank offers twelve comfortable and stylish rooms, with the added attraction of breakfast served in the original bank vault. Reservations: 941–695–3151 or 888–431–1977; e-mail: rents2u@aol.com. *The Ivey House* is a bed and breakfast with family-style "mess hall" breakfast. There are ten rooms plus a cottage. Look for racks of canoes and kayaks and the sign for the Ivey House on your right as you come into Everglades City. The Ivey House also offers kayak rentals, and shuttles both by road and by boat, making a one-way kayaking journey possible (Sandee, at 941–695–3299; e-mail sandee@ivyhouse.com). **CAMPING**   An RV site called *Glades Haven*, across the road from the park entrance in Everglades City, also takes tents. There is a launching ramp and shop. Book a few weeks ahead for a place in January or February.

Route 27:

————————————————————————▶

Turner River Loop

This circular route weaves through delightful mangrove
tunnels up Halfway Creek to Turner Lake and descends
by the wider and more open Turner River to the bay
east of Chokoloskee. There is a choice between two routes
for the return to Everglades City, with one offering a visit to
the historic Smallwood Store.

TRIP HIGHLIGHTS: Very good mangrove tunnels.

TRIP RATING:
   Basic: The route is mostly on sheltered, enclosed water, with few
   opportunities to land.

TRIP DURATION: Half day; about 9 miles, but varies somewhat
   depending on the route options you choose.

NAVIGATION AIDS: Maps of a suitable scale may be obtained at
   the shop at the RV site Glades Haven, across the road from the
   Everglades National Park entrance in Everglades City.

TIDAL INFORMATION: Tide times may be found at the park center. The rising tide flows up to Turner Lake, and the ebb drains
   away from it.

TRIP PLANNING: Use the last of the rising tide to carry you up
   Halfway Creek, and the ebb to carry you down the Turner River. If
   you intend to spend a whole day out, then ideally leave soon after
   low tide. However, it is possible to paddle against the stream.

LAUNCH SITE: From I–75 take exit 14A. Drive south on Route 29
   for 21 miles to Everglades City. Follow the main road through
   town, as if continuing to Chokoloskee. The Everglades National
   Park headquarters is signed to the right, with free parking in the
   vicinity of the park center and a launch ramp to the north side of
   the park building. Parking and launching are free, and no permit
   is required for a day trip. There are alternative parking and

launching sites alongside the causeway between Everglades City and Chokoloskee.

DIRECTIONS

From the park launching ramp, turn left along the shore past the dock until you reach the Route 29 bridge at the start of the causeway (**.5 mile**). Pass under the bridge. There are three visible channels: to right and left and straight ahead. Go straight ahead. This will lead you into Halfway Creek in **half a mile**.

Halfway Creek passes buildings, on your left. Eventually a sign on your right welcomes you to Everglades National Park. From here on you will be on a delightful twisting stream flanked and often tunneled over by mangrove. The route is kept clear of obstacles by means of judicious pruning, but this does not seem to detract from the natural beauty of the mangrove tunnels.

Whenever there is an obvious junction, keep right, until you reach an open patch of water with a crossroads in the waterway. Continue straight ahead. Eventually, after **2.5 miles** on Halfway Creek, you'll reach the broader stretch of water at Turner Lake.

Follow the Turner Lake shore to the right. Islands to your left give the impression you're already on the river, but the entrance to the river is still **half a mile** farther.

As an alternative, make a circuit of the lake, to the left for about **1 mile** before heading into the Left Hand Turner River.

From Turner Lake, follow this fork for **three-quarters of a mile**, to its confluence with the broader, main Turner River. Turn right and continue downstream **1 mile** to the mouth. If you look carefully along the left bank, you should be able to make out the areas of higher ground, now overgrown by vegetation, that are shell mounds left by the Calusa Indians. A complex system of mounds remains in this area.

The town lying ahead is Chokoloskee. Choose between a return to your launch site along the channel to your right, alongside the road on the causeway (**1.5 miles**), and a longer outside route circling Chokoloskee and passing the historic Smallwood Store (**3.5 miles**). The former route will take you back to the bridge, and you will pass under the bridge once

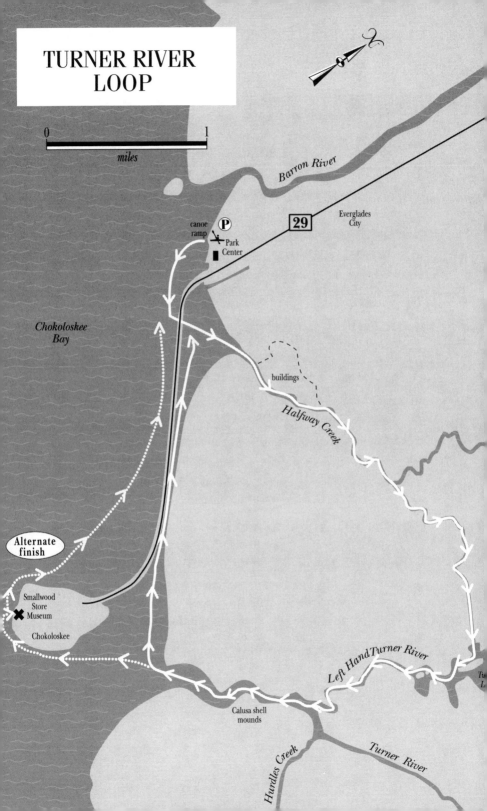

TURNER RIVER LOOP

0   1
miles

Barron River

29

Everglades
City

canoe
ramp **P**
Park
Center

*Chokoloskee
Bay*

buildings

Halfway Creek

**Alternate
finish**

Smallwood
Store
Museum
X

Chokoloskee

Left Hand Turner River

Calusa shell
mounds

Hurdles Creek

Turner River

Hurricane Donna

I sat in the Dip' n Dolphin ice cream parlor in Everglades City and marveled at the cheerfully bright decor: white-painted furniture and walls sponge-splashed with bright acrylics. As an Englishman in Florida, I had melted through the door from the humid sun-beaten tarmac, tempted by a sign that promised coffee and ice cream.

Eventually I found myself chatting with the owner, about Hurricane Donna, which swept through in 1960. She told an incredible tale:

"Trailers were exploding with the gusts of wind. The water was 14 feet deep in the center of Everglades City. All the people went to the courthouse. It was the only building tall enough to be out of the water. We all went upstairs, but soon the water level had reached up to the top floor. Luckily it didn't reach any higher before it began to subside again.

"After the hurricane, a friend asked me about the birds. I suppose they're OK, I said, because I hadn't seen any. Well, that got me thinking! So we went out in our boat to take a look. It was awful!

"Out in the mangroves, all the birds were broken up against the trees, wings and legs all spread out and twisted like pieces of old rag. Poor things never stood a chance. They had nowhere to go. You know, I never thought about the birds until she asked. I suppose I thought they'd be OK, sheltering in the mangroves."

"That was Hurricane Donna!"

more to reach the park center. For the Chokoloskee route, circle the town clockwise until you reach the Smallwood Store in **1 mile**. Landing and launching here is prohibited unless you wish to visit the museum (small entrance fee), which displays the store much as it used to be, along with exhibits showing the Everglades in the early days of white settlement and in the former days of native Indian habitation. You cannot easily miss the brown-painted building raised on pilings on the shore, with its Smallwood Store sign.

From the Smallwood Store, cross the bay (**2.5 miles**) to finish at the park center.

Where to Eat & Where to Stay

For information on lodging, camping, and restaurants, see the section on where to eat and where to stay for Route 26, Everglades City Circuit.

Route 28:

━━ ━━ ━━ ━━ ━━ ━━ ━━ ━━ ━━ ━━ ━━ ━━ ➤

Turner River from Tamiami Trail

The Turner River is an easy trip leading from the Tamiami Trail (U.S. 41) to the town of Everglades City. The descent, although there is scarcely a gradient, begins on freshwater and ends in saltwater estuary. You will pass a significant cluster of Calusa Indian shell mounds.

TRIP HIGHLIGHTS: Freshwater Everglades stream leading to sheltered tidal water. Great trip for seeing birds.

TRIP RATING:
   Basic

TRIP DURATION: Half day (3–4 hours); 9.5 miles.

NAVIGATION AIDS: USGS 1:24,000 topographic maps "Ochopee" and "Chokoloskee."

TIDAL INFORMATION: The freshwater flows downstream but not fast. The saltwater part is gently tidal but there is little stream.

TRIP PLANNING: Plan your trip to begin at the time of high water at Chokoloskee. Then when you reach saltwater, you will benefit from paddling with the falling tide. If you need a shuttle for this one-way trip, contact Ivey House (see page 150).

LAUNCH SITE: Start at the junction of State Road 839 and U.S. 41 (the Tamiami Trail). The route got the name Tamiami Trail because it links Tampa and Miami. You will finish at the park center at Everglades City, or on the Chokoloskee Causeway beside State Road 29.

Reminders of the Past

The Turner River is named after Captain Dick Turner, the first white settler at Chokoloskee. Turner served as a scout in the Third Seminole War, in the 1850s. Chokoloskee and the lower part of the Turner River appear to have been important sites for the Calusa Indians.

The Chokoloskee site is built on an island, once covering 105 acres, almost 80 percent of which consisted of Indian accumulations of seashells built into ridges and mounds. A steep-sided tower of shells some 27 feet high, and measuring 90 feet by 25 feet at the base, once stood at one corner of the island. The tower may have once served as a temple.

Most of the shell mounds were flattened this century to provide sites for building. However, there are still twenty-eight shell mounds in a complex on the southeast side of Turner River just upstream from its mouth, thought to date from about A.D. 200 to A.D. 900. These mounds form a series of ridges and valleys in what must have been a carefully planned pattern. The valleys may have served as canals for dugouts.

At intervals upstream for more than 9 miles are more shell mounds. But it's easy to descend the river without noticing a single mound, because they are almost completely hidden by mangrove. But for hundreds of years, this was a significant center for fishing and trade for the Calusas.

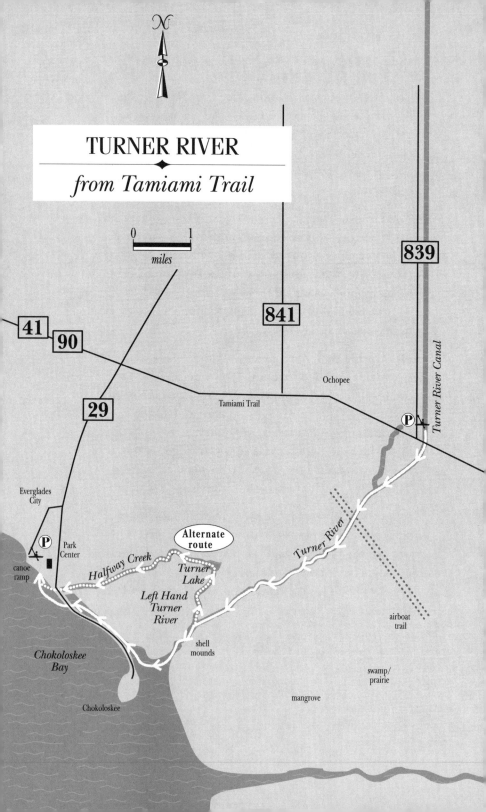

TURNER RIVER
from Tamiami Trail

N

0   1
miles

839

841

41

90

29

Ochopee

Tamiami Trail

Turner River Canal

P

Everglades
City

P

Park
Center

canoe
ramp

Halfway Creek

**Alternate
route**

*Turner
Lake*

*Left Hand
Turner
River*

Turner River

airboat
trail

shell
mounds

*Chokoloskee
Bay*

swamp/
prairie

mangrove

Chokoloskee

Launch at the southwest (downstream) side of the bridge that is close to the road junction, across the road from H.P. Williams Park. You'll be in the Turner River Canal, which after about **1.5 miles** joins the Turner River. The vegetation is saw grass and reeds, typical of the freshwater Everglades.

Keep left of the islands of trees. An airboat trail crosses the route (**2 miles** from start), after which you should keep to the main flow of water which passes beneath mangroves and is joined by two small tributaries, from right and then from left (about **4 miles** from start). From here on, the river becomes wider until it is joined in another **2 miles** by the Left

Hand Turner River, which runs in from the right. Continue down the Turner River for **1 mile** to its mouth. On the way, look for overgrown banks up to 20 feet high on the left side of the river. Together these make up a complex series of Calusa shell mounds.

At the river mouth, turn right and follow the shore for **half a mile** to the canal running alongside the Chokoloskee Causeway. Either land on the causeway at a suitable spot or continue alongside the causeway until you

Turner River from Tamiami Trail

reach the bridge beneath it (**1.5 miles**). Paddle under the bridge, to Chokoloskee Bay. Keep right for another **half mile** to return to the canoe ramp just beyond the marina and the park office.

ROUTE ALTERNATIVE: At the junction of the main Turner River and the Left Hand of Turner River, turn right and follow the Left Hand to Turner Lake (**.75 mile**). Keep left here and skirt the shore to find the opening to Halfway Creek (**.5 mile**). Or it's about **a mile** if you wish to circle the lake, to the right.

Follow Halfway Creek, which is narrow and often enclosed above with vegetation. At the one obvious crossroads, go straight ahead. Otherwise keep left at any junction.

You'll pass buildings and narrow canals to your right (**2 miles** from Turner Lake) as you approach Everglades City. You'll reach open water after another **half mile** and see the Chokoloskee Causeway ahead.

Now either cross to the causeway to land and leave the water, or paddle under the bridge and turn right. Paddle **half a mile**, past the entrance to the marina, to land at the park center canoe ramp.

Where to Eat & Where to Stay

For information on lodging, camping, and restaurants, see the section on where to eat and where to stay Route 26, Everglades City Circuit.

Route 29:

▬ ▬ ▬ ▬ ▬ ▬ ▬ ▬ ▬ ▬ ▬ ▬ ➤

Picnic Key

This day-trip starts at Everglades City and crosses Chokoloskee Bay to a channel between the many mangrove keys to the west. The destination is a great lunch spot on Picnic Key at the western fringe of this mangrove archipelago, a little over 6 miles from Everglades City.

Picnic Key features long, sandy beaches and views of lone mangrove trees on sand banks, and presents a striking contrast to the enclosed atmosphere deeper between the islands.

TRIP HIGHLIGHTS: Long sandy beaches lining the Mangrove Keys.

TRIP RATING:
Basic/Intermediate: This trip offers a wilderness feel.

TRIP DURATION: One day; 12 miles round trip.

NAVIGATION AIDS: Waterproof Charts #41; NOAA chart #11430.

TIDAL INFORMATION: Paddle out to Picnic Key on a falling tide and return on a rising tide, if possible. Launch from Everglades City with at least two hours of remaining falling tide.(For example, if high water is at 9:00 A.M., launch between 9:00 A.M. and 1:00 P.M.) The tidal streams will give you quite a lot of assistance. There's not much more than 4 feet of tidal range, but a lot of water drains through these narrow channels.

CAUTIONS: Indian Key Pass carries a lot of small boat traffic at times. It can be safer and more relaxing if you keep to the side of the marked channel. The route will take you out from the shelter of the keys onto the open Gulf coast, where wave conditions may be different. Check at the Everglades National Park office by the launch ramp for likely conditions before you set out.

TRIP PLANNING: Check at the park office to make certain Picnic Key is still open to the public. Access to popular keys is sometimes restricted for a period to give relief from detrimental impact. You'll also find the tide times and weather forecast here.

LAUNCH SITE: From I–75 take exit 14A. Drive south on Route 29 for 21 miles to Everglades City. Follow the main road through town, as if continuing to Chokoloskee. The Everglades National Park headquarters is signed to the right. Park free in the vicinity of the park center. Launching from the site north of the park building is free.

 **DIRECTIONS**

Cross Chokoloskee Bay in a roughly southwest direction to the entrance to Indian Key Pass (**1 mile**), a channel identified by navigation marks. From a distance, watch for boats entering and emerging from the entrance, which will help you pinpoint its position. We saw manatees close to this entrance.

Follow Indian Key Pass for **3.5 miles** to Indian Key. The current may be swift, so keep your distance from the upstream end of mangroves and spoil islands (islands composed of dredged material). We saw dolphins in this channel.

From Indian Key, Picnic Key lies **1.5 miles** to the northwest. If you need a sheltered landing, look between Tiger Key and Picnic Key.

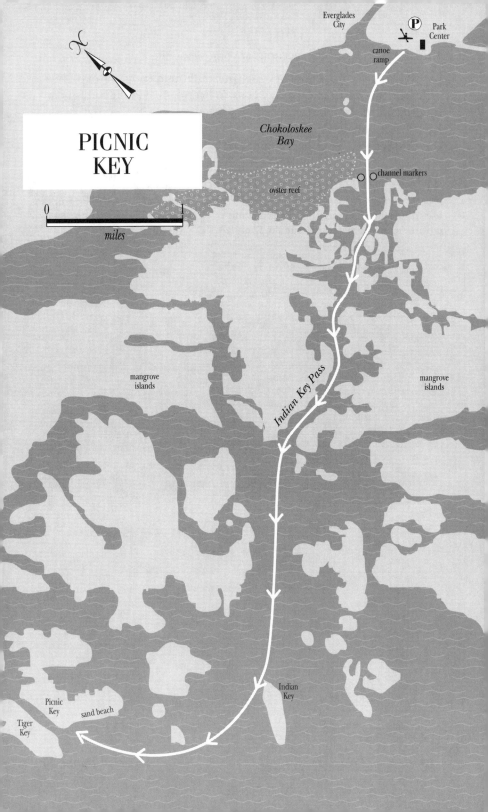

PICNIC KEY

Everglades City

P Park Center

canoe ramp

Chokoloskee Bay

○ ○ channel markers

oyster reef

0   1

miles

mangrove islands

Indian Key Pass

mangrove islands

Indian Key

Picnic Key

sand beach

Tiger Key

CAUTION: Watch out for raccoons at your picnic site.

On your return trip, either reverse your outbound route, or explore a different (maybe quieter) route back to Everglades City. If you keep a roughly northeast course through the islands, you will eventually emerge back into Chokoloskee Bay, where you should be able to see Everglades City and return to your starting point.

Where to Eat & Where to Stay

For information on lodging, camping, and restaurants, see the section on where to eat and where to stay for Route 26, Everglades City Circuit.

Route 30:

▬▬ ▬▬ ▬▬ ▬▬ ▬▬ ▬▬ ▬▬ ▬▬ ▬▬ ▬▬ ▬▬ ➡

Hells Bay

This trip in Everglades National Park explores an area of mangrove forest that opens up with distance from the launch site into a bewildering area of streams and ponds, but still offers protection from the wind. It is a way-marked route, which makes navigation along the narrow channels considerably easier than it might otherwise appear, but use of a compass will also help.

There are three round-trip options of varying length, each to either a primitive camping site or a chickee (camping platform). You can overnight at these places, cutting your mileage, but you must purchase a backcountry permit prior to starting if you wish to camp. Registration for a backcountry permit must be made at the Visitors Center in Flamingo up until twenty-four hours before the day on which your trip begins (941–695–2945).

TRIP HIGHLIGHTS: Easily followed system of markers through sheltered ponds and streams in a mangrove forest.

TRIP RATING:
   Basic: Fascinating area!

TRIP DURATION: 8 hours, 12 miles for the round-trip to Hells Bay. For a shorter option, travel only as far as Pearl Bay: 6 hours; 8 miles round-trip. For the shortest option, travel only as far as Lard Can, a tent site: 4 hours; 6 miles, round-trip.

   Each of the three destinations offers limited camping facilities. This trip also includes an option for additional paddling beyond Hells Bay, going for 8.5 miles from Hells Bay to Flamingo.

NAVIGATION AIDS: Waterproof Charts #39; NOAA chart #11433.

TIDAL INFORMATION: Much of the trip is on nontidal water, with a slow current, and the tidal effect elsewhere is insignificant.

TRIP PLANNING: Landing in the mangroves is difficult, but there are toilet facilities at the campsites on the route. Carry bug repellent.

LAUNCH SITE: Follow State Road 27 (Ingraham Highway), the main park road, 8 miles north from the Park Office at Flamingo until you see a brown canoe sign to the left of the road. The sign indicates your launch site.

DIRECTIONS

Numbered white poles indicate the route, so follow the rising numbers on your outward journey and the decreasing numbers on your way back. Launch on the north side of the road at the small dock, and follow the route as it winds through mangroves. The waterway widens past marker 154, shortly before the Lard Can camp site, which is on dry land, **3 miles** from the launch site.

From Lard Can to Pearl Bay at marker 167, the **1-mile-long** route passes through a series of channels and bays. There is a double chickee at Pearl Bay.

Channels and bays of similar nature follow for the **2 miles** from Pearl Bay to the double chickee camping facility at Hell's Bay, marker 174.

ADDITIONAL PADDLING (intermediate): You can extend this trip if you'd like, turning it into a **14.5-mile** one-way journey from your original launch site to Flamingo.

This alternative links Hells Bay to Whitewater Bay and the southern end of the Wilderness Waterway. Hells Bay to Flamingo is about **8.5 miles**, with easy navigation once you reach Whitewater Bay.

Follow the East River from Hell's Bay to Whitewater Bay (**1.5 miles**).

Follow the shore of Whitewater Bay southwest to the mouth of Tarpon Creek (**2.5 miles**). The creek is marked as part of the Wilderness Waterway, and you'll probably also see boats appearing from or disappearing into the creek.

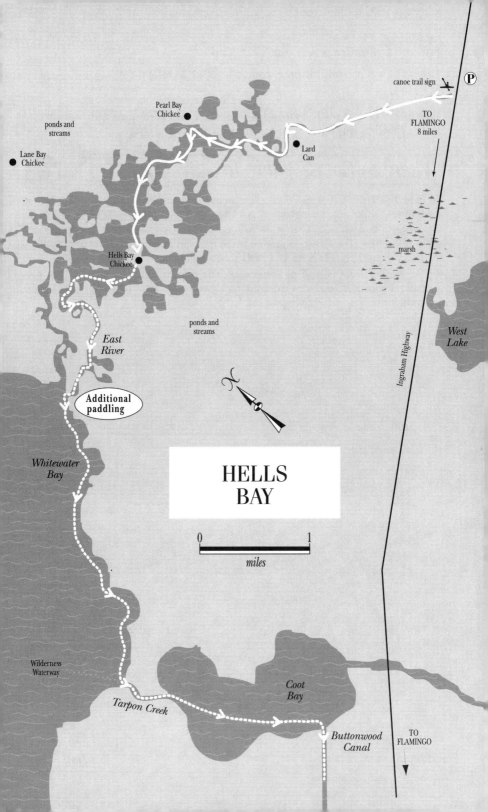

canoe trail sign

P

Pearl Bay
Chickee

ponds and
streams

Lane Bay
Chickee

Lard
Can

TO
FLAMINGO
8 miles

marsh

Hells Bay
Chickee

West
Lake

ponds and
streams

East
River

Ingraham Highway

Additional
paddling

HELLS
BAY

Whitewater
Bay

0   1

miles

Wilderness
Waterway

Coot
Bay

Tarpon Creek

Buttonwood
Canal

TO
FLAMINGO

Follow Tarpon Creek to Coot Bay (**.5 mile**).

Cross Coot Bay to the Buttonwood Canal (**1.5 miles**), following the markers.

Paddle down the Buttonwood Canal to its end (**2.5 miles**) at the tidal barrier beside the parking area and marina in Flamingo.

Where to Eat & Where to Stay

RESTAURANTS   The restaurant at Flamingo serves breakfast, lunch and dinner, while snacks are served at the ground level lounge. **LODGING** *Flamingo Lodge* offers motel rooms and housekeeping cottages, call (800–600–3813). For all accommodations in the National Park, call (800) 600–3813 or (941) 695–3101. **CAMPING**   The campground at Flamingo has barbecue stands, showers, and pleasant sites. The bugs in the area are notorious in summer. Follow the road west from the park center and you'll drive into the campground.

Route 31:

━ ━ ━ ━ ━ ━ ━ ━ ━ ━ ━ ━ ━ ━ ━ ➤

Cape Sable

For a strenuous three- or four-day paddling adventure, try this journey that circles Cape Sable at the northwest corner of Florida Bay.

The four-day trip comprises a two-day journey from Flamingo along the Gulf coastline followed by a two-day cruise around the perimeter of Whitewater Bay, a saline lake surrounded by mangrove and peppered with mangrove islands.

The three-day alternative for the more energetic paddler completes this last section in a single one-day stretch, either following the route around the perimeter of Whitewater Bay or tracing a route straight across the bay from island to island in more open and exposed waters.

TRIP HIGHLIGHTS: Classic Everglades wilderness paddling with scenery from shallow Florida Bay waters to deeper exposed sandy shores of the Gulf of Mexico, between mangrove islands into increasingly less saline conditions to finish in the Buttonwood Canal in conditions more typical of a Florida stream with alligators and woodland.

TRIP RATING:

Advanced: Paddling the outer coast is committing, with exposure to the Gulf. Although these waters may be calm, waves sometimes hit several feet in height, and no sheltered landing is available. Winds across Whitewater Bay generally produce a short chop, and it can be hard work to paddle against the wind in the open water. No one lives within this area, and there's no way out of it except at the camping sites permitted by park authorities. Tides run swiftly through the passes, requiring sustained powerful paddling whenever you find yourself going against the tide. You will need to carry all your supplies with you for camping.

TRIP DURATION: Three to four days; 52 miles.

DAY 1: FLAMINGO TO MIDDLE CAPE; 14 miles.

DAY 2: MIDDLE CAPE TO GRAVEYARD CREEK; 14 miles.

DAY 3: GRAVEYARD CREEK TO JOE RIVER CHICKEE; 9 miles.

DAY 4: JOE RIVER CHICKEE TO FLAMINGO; 15 miles

ALTERNATIVE FINISH: Days three and four can be combined into one day, for a total trip duration of three days. This final day measures 22 miles across Whitewater Bay or 24 miles via the Joe River.

NAVIGATION AIDS: Waterproof Charts #39; NOAA chart #11433

TIDAL INFORMATION: The range is less than 6 feet. The tidal stream pushes inland on the flood and ebbs to the coast.

CAUTIONS: This is a wilderness route where you will be far from help. Take provisions to be self-sufficient in case of an emergency.

TRIP PLANNING: Plan your trip for the period between early November and late March. Outside of this period, the bugs can be horrendous. Pick a period when low tide is in the morning, ideally around 9:00 or 10:00 A.M. This will give you the assistance of the tidal stream around the coast during comfortable paddling hours. The bugs are at their most voracious during early morning and through the evening, so be prepared to move fast if you start early.

A Guy Named Guy

Bradley Key is named after Guy Bradley who grew up in the late nineteenth century in the Palm Beach area and made a living for a time collecting egret plumes for the manufacturers of women's hats and for hair ornaments. Egret plumes demanded a higher price per ounce than gold. After the devastation of whole rookeries of birds, slaughtered solely for their plumes, Florida outlawed plume hunting in 1901.

Bradley switched roles and became a bird warden for the National Association of Audubon Societies, protecting birds in the area around the tip of Florida. He was murdered in 1905 while trying to arrest poachers. Although the man charged in his death was later acquitted, Bradley's murder widened national awareness of the need for bird protection.

Bradley's grave was washed away in 1960 by Hurricane Donna, which simultaneously obliterated the bird colony he was trying to protect when he was killed.

LAUNCH SITE: The road to Flamingo from Florida City is the only road crossing the Everglades in this area. An entrance fee ($10 for a car for a period up to six days) is payable at the Everglades National Park entrance, some 27 miles from Flamingo. The Rangers Office is situated in Flamingo in the large building at the end of the road. You'll find little else. The only inhabitants are park and concession employees and their families. Pick up a backcountry camping permit at the Rangers Office (another $10). This is good for a multiday journey and for a party of up to six. There are two launching ramps in the marina area: one into Florida Bay, the other into Buttonwood Canal, which links Flamingo to Whitewater Bay. (The exit from the canal into Florida Bay is blocked by a barrier to keep salinity in the canal low.) This paddling trip begins on the Florida Bay ramp—and ends three or four days later at the Buttonwood Canal ramp.

DAY 1: FLAMINGO TO MIDDLE CAPE (14 miles)

Paddle from the sheltered marina area at Flamingo and turn right (west). For the **first mile** or so you will be in an area of scattered mangrove keys (islands). The water is shallow and often murky, so be alert here for signs of shallows you cannot cross.

Mangrove shoots and wading birds such as herons and ibis offer an indication of water depth. Rays and other fish abound, although the water can be so murky it can be impossible to see what you have disturbed as you pass. A violent eruption of water could be a large ray or a nurse shark.

After another **1.5 miles**, you'll go pass Bradley Key.

The East Clubhouse campsite is situated about **2 miles** past Bradley Key.

Clubhouse Beach Campsite is beyond the next low point of land, marked by a signpost above the beach (**5 miles** from Bradley Key). The shore is blue clay here, but firm enough to walk over, with flat dryland beyond.

From here the shore consists of mangrove, but by East Cape (**2.75 miles** beyond Clubhouse Beach), the mangroves are replaced by a steep, sandy shore made of broken shell, backed by palms and pines and other trees, plus cactus and areas of grasses. A sandy spit at East Cape can produce a small tide race, so keep close to shore if the tide is running against you. Stakes protruding from the water by the shore a few yards farther down the beach are remains of an old dock. This is a good place to stretch your legs and to look at the seashells and sponges washed onto the shore.

Middle Cape is the next prominent point ahead (**4 miles** beyond East Cape), in a generally northwesterly direction. Follow the curve of the shell beach. The mangroves at Middle Cape grow through the sand, not through mud, so it's easy to walk between them and look at them without getting your feet wet. Find a suitable camping spot for the night. The top of the sand beach can be fine if sea conditions are calm.

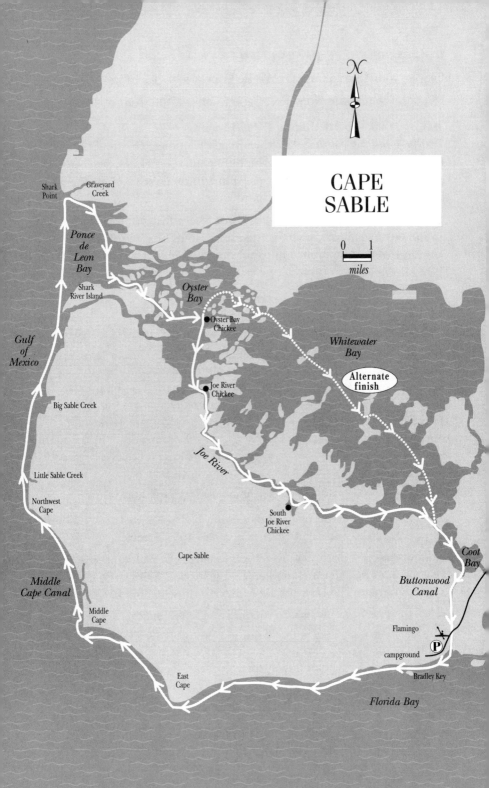

CAPE
SABLE

0   1
miles

Shark
Point
Graveyard
Creek

Ponce
de
Leon
Bay

Shark
River Island

Oyster
Bay

Oyster Bay
Chickee

Whitewater
Bay

Alternate
finish

Gulf
of
Mexico

Big Sable Creek

Joe River
Chickee

Joe River

Little Sable Creek

Northwest
Cape

South
Joe River
Chickee

Cape Sable

Coot
Bay

Middle
Cape Canal

Buttonwood
Canal

Middle
Cape

Flamingo

campground

P

Bradley Key

East
Cape

Florida Bay

DAY 2: *MIDDLE CAPE TO GRAVEYARD CREEK* (**14 miles**)

Paddle from Middle Cape to Middle Cape Canal (**1.5 miles**).

From the canal until Northwest Cape (**3 miles**), the shore is predominantly mangrove.

Paddle from Northwest Cape to Little Sable Creek, a distance of **1 mile**.

It's **2 miles** from Little Sable Creek to Big Sable Creek, where you'll find a bay three-quarters of a mile wide, with a number of creeks leading from the mangroves.

The route from Big Sable Creek to Little Shark River (**2.5 miles**) follows an indented mangrove coast. The western point of Shark River Island juts out from the coast, making a prominent target. There is a green light off the western tip of the island. (Little Shark River extends northwest from there.)

From the light, Shark Point is in line of sight across Ponce de Leon Bay (**3.75 miles** away, at a true bearing of 10 degrees). However, the features of Graveyard Creek are difficult to identify at this range.

From the light, either follow the curve of Ponce de Leon Bay for **5.5 miles** or cross the bay direct (**3.75 miles**). Here you'll find a small creek—Graveyard Creek—running into a small bay from the mangroves. There is more than one possible landing west of the creek onto the small camping area signed as Graveyard Creek, your home for the night. Here is a picnic table, a toilet, and coconut palms. Pelicans dive close to the point.

DAY 3: *GRAVEYARD CREEK TO JOE RIVER CHICKEE* (**9 miles**)

Return to the south across Ponce de Leon Bay to the east end of Shark River Island (**2.5 miles** at a bearing of about 155 degrees).

Now follow the shore eastward for **1 mile** until you pick up the line of U.S. Coast Guard channel markers that lead for **2 miles** to Oyster Bay. The tidal stream can be quite swift through these channels.

Cross for **1 mile** to the eastern side of Oyster Bay and locate Oyster Bay Chickee. The chickee is situated at the southwest end of an island that lies half a mile south of the marked channel across Oyster Bay but is hidden from view by a belt of mangroves.

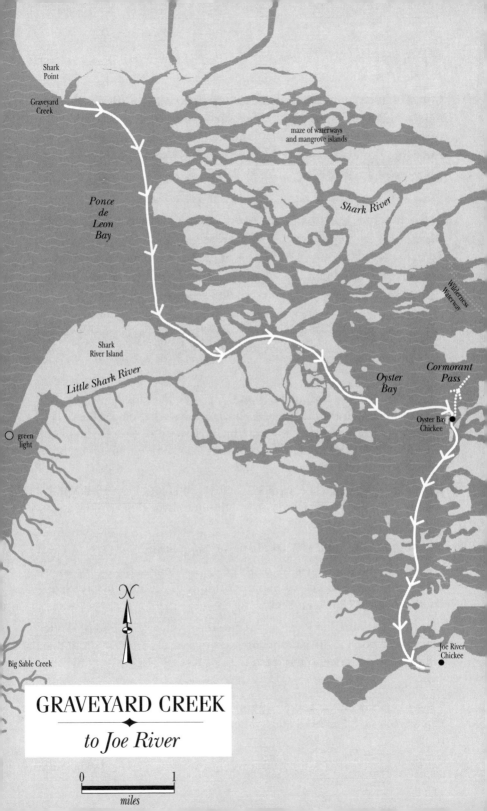

Shark
Point

Graveyard
Creek

maze of waterways
and mangrove islands

*Ponce
de
Leon
Bay*

Shark River

Wilderness Waterway

Shark
River
Island

Little Shark River

*Oyster
Bay*

*Cormorant
Pass*

Oyster Bay
Chickee

○ green
light

N

Big Sable Creek

Joe River
Chickee

GRAVEYARD CREEK
◆
to Joe River

0 ⸻ 1

miles

Fear

Coconut palms, with their abundant tough roots, can often withstand hurricanes. People are said to have survived hurricanes by lashing themselves to coconut palms. If you tried this at the Graveyard Creek campsite, you would more likely be drowned by the storm surge, which can exceed 20 feet.

As the three of us sat at a picnic table in the half-light imagining the power of a hurricane and watching the bright flashes of evening fireflies flitting through the trees, Robert noticed a pale shape emerging from between the boards of the tabletop. It moved ghostlike across our cutlery, legs spanning wide. But we focused on the scorpion's long tail. Without a word, three pairs of elbows retreated from the tabletop and three pairs of bare knees slid out from beneath the table, where simultaneously we had each imagined more scorpions to be lurking.

Oyster Bay Chickee is more open to the breeze than the Graveyard Creek campsite and thus can make a welcome resting place. There is a toilet. If the early morning bugs are bad at Graveyard Creek, you might consider a late breakfast at the Oyster Bay Chickee when the bugs have settled down a bit.

From Oyster Bay Chickee, explore the eastern coast of Oyster Bay to its southeastern extremity. Here you will find Joe River Chickee, the stopping place for your third night.

DAY 4: JOE RIVER CHICKEE TO FLAMINGO (15 miles)

Follow the winding course of Joe River south, then southeast, for about **5.5 miles**, where you will have an opportunity to get out and stretch at South Joe River Chickee.

East from here the Joe River opens into the southeastern end of Whitewater Bay. Look for the channel markers tucked close to the shore that indicate the entrance to the canal to Coot Bay.

The channel to Coot Bay is only half a mile long.

Cross Coot Bay (**1.5 miles**) to Buttonwood Canal, which leads back to Flamingo. The **2.5-mile** canal is rather straight, and subject to boat traffic.

You will know your journey is reaching its end when you reach the road bridge. The exit ramp is on your right, a few yards before the concession buildings and the concrete barrier that blocks the canal.

THE THREE-DAY ALTERNATIVE TRIP: To reduce this trip to three days, start by following the schedule for Days 1 and 2. For your third and final day, simply combine the schedule for Days 3 and 4—paddling all the way from Graveyard Creek to Flamingo in a single push.

For this final day, you have a choice of routes, depending on wind direction and strength. You can simply take the enclosed route through the mangrove channel of the Joe River, as described under Days 3 and 4. Or you can take the Day 3 route only as far as Oyster Bay Chickee, and then turn northerly to join the Wilderness Waterway route, which offers open water with a wide panorama of distant mangroves and occasional mangrove islands.

FOR THE WILDERNESS WATERWAY OPTION, follow the Oyster Bay coast north from Oyster Bay Chickee to the channel markers in Oyster Bay (about **three-quarters of a mile** to red marker #50). From here paddle at a bearing of 120 degrees into Cormorant Pass. You'll then pick up a string of navigation marks that will guide you from here to Flamingo.

Once in Whitewater Bay, follow an approximate course of 140 degrees. This route follows the middle of Whitewater Bay, crossing from island to island.

Coot Bay

Coot Bay is named after the freshwater birds that used to live here in large numbers. The coot looks a bit like a black duck with a white patch above the bill, and it pumps its head forward and back as it swims. The Buttonwood Canal let in saltwater from Florida Bay that destroyed the habitat required by the coots. The more recent plugging of the canal at the Florida Bay end is gradually restoring the former conditions, and you will probably see some of these birds.

The entrance to the **half-mile-long** canal that runs from the southeast corner of Whitewater Bay into Coot Bay is indicated by channel markers and posts, but you can spot it from a greater distance if you watch where other boat traffic goes.

Paddle the **1.5 miles** across Coot Bay to Buttonwood Canal, and then it's just **2.5 miles** down the canal to your finishing point at Flamingo.

Where to Eat & Where to Stay

RESTAURANTS There is a restaurant and bar in the main park building. **LODGING AND CAMPING** *The Flamingo Lodge and Cabins* and a neighboring campground, both west of the Rangers Office, are your options in Flamingo, with the nearest alternatives being outside the park. For information about the accommodations in the park, phone (800) 600–3813 or (941) 695–3101. Hot showers are available for a fee in the marina building close to the landing ramp, from 10:00 A.M. to 3:00 P.M. There are cold showers in the campground.

Route 32:

--➤

Nest Keys

This journey follows a sheltered route from Key Largo through Tarpon Basin and Little Buttonwood Sound to Porjoe Key, an excellent bird-watching area. From Porjoe there is an open crossing of about 2 miles to the Nest Keys, notable as one of the best places in the keys to see roseate spoonbills. The route crosses into Everglades National Park.

Depending on wind conditions, you have two alternative routes back: the reverse of the outward route, or via the Boggies into Blackwater Sound to then either cut directly across the sound to your starting point or to follow the southern shore back.

TRIP HIGHLIGHTS: A great area for birdwatching.

TRIP RATING:
Intermediate: An enclosed route, but it seems open!

TRIP DURATION: Full day; 15 miles. You can also arrange to camp on North Nest Key, dividing the trip into two halves of about **7.5 miles** each. (See Route 33, Nest Keys Overnight, for a day trip from the camp site on North Nest Key to the northern coast of Florida Bay.)

NAVIGATION AIDS: Large-print Waterproof Charts #33E.

TIDAL INFORMATION: Tidal range negligible.

TRIP PLANNING: Check the weather. You'll be away from civilization, so take chart and compass. If you become lost, head southeast for the road. It's worth taking binoculars to watch the birds, but you'll need to keep them dry.

Spoonbills and Flamingos

Seeing a flock of roseate spoonbills is one of those truly magical Floridian experiences: plumage of coral pink with a blushing red splash at the shoulder, viewed in the context of shallow waters of jade and turquoise, with clear blue sky above. If you could wish for a perfect dessert, this would be it. Never mind the Key lime pie!

The spoonbill has a bill that's flattened top to bottom, which distinguishes it from any other wading bird. Immature spoonbills are white, only acquiring the pink color with age. The bird feeds by swishing its beak from side to side in the water.

The only other bird that's a vibrant pink is the flamingo. There's a similarity of color that at a distance could confuse you, but the flamingo is seldom seen nowadays. That is, in its live form: The ubiquitous "garden flamingo" found wire-legged and bulbous-billed in gardens throughout the U.S. ridicules the glowing plumage of a bird that once was far more widespread in Southern Florida than in Seattle yards. I only hope that one day the flamingo will return in flocks to these waters and enrich the scene in a similar way to the spoonbills.

LAUNCH SITE: From U.S. 1 south from Homestead, cross Florida Bay until you reach the right-angle turn at Key Largo. From here, Florida Bay Outfitters is just under 2.5 miles southwest on U.S. 1, to the right of the road, marked by a tall yellow kayak standing on end. Park to the north of the shop. Launching is free from the sandy beach adjacent to the parking lot. The staff at Florida Bay Outfitters is friendly and helpful, able to give excellent local advice.

DIRECTIONS

From the beach, follow the shore to your left (southwest) until you meet the marked boat channel through Dusenbury Creek (**1.5 miles**).

Paddle through the creek, which splits into several channels suitable for

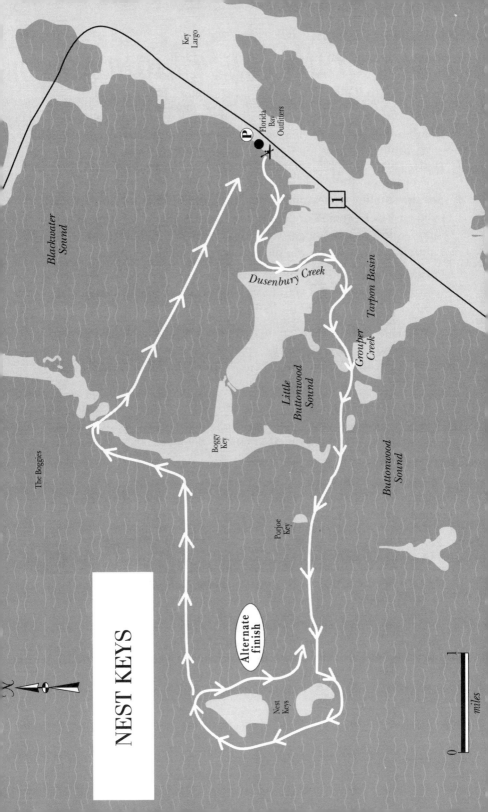

NEST KEYS

Key Largo

Florida Bay Outfitters

P

1

Blackwater Sound

Dusenbury Creek

Tarpon Basin

Grouper Creek

Little Buttonwood Sound

Boggy Key

Buttonwood Sound

The Boggies

Porjoe Key

Alternate finish

Nest Keys

0   miles   1

a kayak (**1 mile**). On reaching Tarpon Basin follow the coast to your right (curving north, west, then south) to Grouper Creek, or cross directly west (**.6 mile** to **1.5 miles** depending on your exit from Dusenbury Creek and your route in Tarpon Basin).

Part way through Grouper Creek is a channel to your right (**.2 mile**) leading into Little Buttonwood Sound. Pass through this gap (**100 yards**), turn left, and keep to the south of the bay until you can choose a way through to Buttonwood Sound. Follow the string of keys almost northwest to the westernmost tip of Boggy Key, **1.1 miles** from the exit from Grouper Creek. Porjoe Key lies almost **1 mile** to the west of the westernmost point of Boggy Key. (Boggy Key is reputedly named after Humphrey Bogart, who was filmed here in *The African Queen*.)

Porjoe Key is a good area for bird-watching. Roseate spoonbills may be seen here, although the Nest Keys, **2 miles** almost due west and a little north of west, are better known for these birds.

From the Nest Keys, return either by reversing your outward journey or, from the northernmost Nest Key, paddle due east (**2.6 miles**) until you reach Boggy Key. Then follow the coast north for about **1 mile** until you find a channel into Blackwater Sound.

There are several channels here, known as The Boggies, each about .3 mile long. Now you'll know, if you wondered before, why the *African Queen* scenes of the boat mired in endless flat-water channels were filmed here.

Once you reach Blackwater Sound, your original launch site should be visible across the water (**3 miles**), but if in doubt follow the shore of the sound to the south until you reach your car.

Where to Eat & Where to Stay

RESTAURANTS   Try the *Caribbean Club* next to your parking spot. For the *Flamingo Restaurant*, turn right just before the big bend in I-5 going north (mile marker 106.5, on the oceanside) on the water in Garden Cove (305–451–8022). **LODGINGS**   For local kayaking-friendly accommodations, try those offered by Jamie Jackson (305–451–9968; e-mail fbokayak@aol.com). Jamie also runs kayak tours in the area. **CAMPING** For information on camping overnight on North Nest Key, call Everglades National Park (941–695–2945). Also see further information in Route 33, Nest Keys Overnight.

Route 33:

━━ ━━ ━━ ━━ ━━ ━━ ━━ ━━ ━━ ━━ ━ ➤

Nest Keys Overnight

Starting from Nest Keys, this trip takes you on an 11-mile round trip to the southern fringes of the Everglades. You may even see the rare American crocodile.

To get to Nest Keys in the first place, just follow the directions for Route 32, Nest Keys.

The beach camping site at North Nest Key is managed by Everglades National Park. Register by phone for the required backcountry permit (941–695–2945). Registration will not be accepted until within 24 hours of the start of your trip. For bird-watchers, this camp makes an ideal base, with a maximum permitted stay of seven nights.

TRIP HIGHLIGHTS: The possibility of seeing a crocodile, the certainty of watching birds, and the solitude of a whole day at least 4 miles from the nearest road.

TRIP RATING:
Intermediate: A great getaway.

TRIP DURATION: Full day; 11 miles. Allow 5 hours of paddling time.

NAVIGATION AIDS: Large-print Waterproof Chart #33E; NOAA chart #11452.

TIDAL INFORMATION: Insignificant tides.

CAUTIONS: Carry emergency equipment and a weather radio.

TRIP PLANNING: You'll need a map and compass. You will also need to carry all your food and water requirements for your stay.

LAUNCH SITE: Follow the launch and paddling directions for Trip Nest Keys, to get to the start of this trip at North Nest Key.

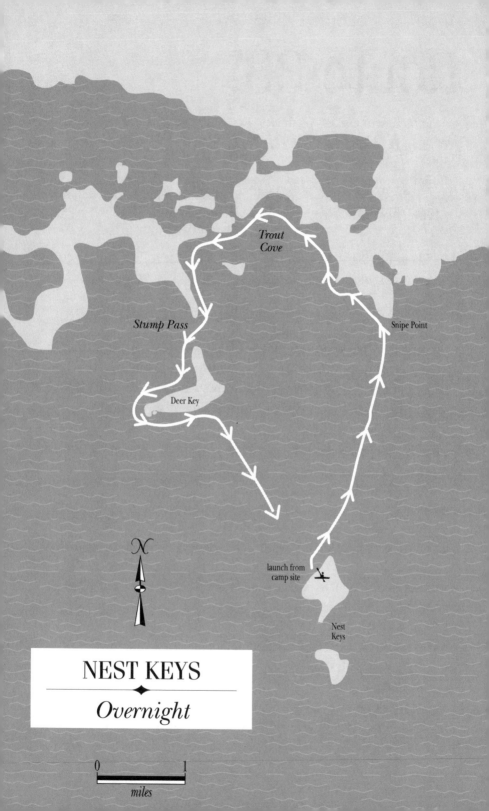

Trout
Cove

Stump Pass

Snipe Point

Deer Key

launch from
camp site

Nest
Keys

N

NEST KEYS

Overnight

0   1
miles

DIRECTIONS

Start at the north end of North Nest Key. Snipe Point lies about **2.75 miles** away on a bearing of approximately 20 degrees. Cross to Snipe Point.

Follow the shore northwest from Snipe Point into Trout Cove and explore the cove. The shoreline extends about **3.5 miles**. This is an area where you may be lucky enough to see a crocodile.

The area north of Trout Cove is a designated wildlife protection area, closed to public access.

At the southwestern end of Trout Cove is a point, beyond which is Deer Key, separated from the point by quarter-mile-wide Stump Pass. Explore the coast of Deer Key in a counterclockwise direction.

Return from here to North Nest Key, which lies southeast of Deer Key at a distance of about **2.5 miles**.

Where to Eat & Where to Stay

CAMPING Camping is your only option on Nest Keys. (See the registration details earlier in this chapter.) Your dining opportunities here are limited to the food you bring with you, your imagination, and your cooking ability. (Caviar, avocado, and Brie with crackers and a glass of wine for starters?)

Crocodiles

Crocodiles are not very common in the United States—only an estimated six hundred found only in and around Florida Bay. You are far more likely to see an alligator—but to tell the two apart, look for the crocodile's narrower snout.

If you do see a crocodile, treat it with respect, but be reassured that this is not the overtly aggressive marine crocodile found elsewhere in the world, as in Crocodile Dundee. This tropical estuarine crocodile is one of the most docile of the crocodiles, attaining a length of up to about 12 feet but eating mostly fish, crabs, and snakes.

Although crocodiles are seldom seen, one man told me how he walked to the waterfront on his property at Key Largo to see a large croc lying in the sun, a few yards away, right up on his neighbor's dock.

Route 34:

El Radabob Key

El Radabob Key lies on the Atlantic side of Key Largo. A complete circuit of El Radabob Key totals about 12 miles, but the nature of the sheltered waters with mangrove channels at either end of Largo Sound, and the good bird-watching, make a much shorter trip attractive too. The shorter route I suggest offers about 4 miles of sheltered paddling.

TRIP HIGHLIGHTS: Bird-watching in mangrove channels, with the option of some paddling on more exposed coast.

TRIP RATING:
Basic: Good variety.

TRIP DURATION: Full circuit: 5 hours; 12 miles. Shorter route: Paddle to the north end of Largo Sound and return, 2 hours; 4 miles.

NAVIGATION AIDS: Waterproof Charts #33; NOAA chart #11463.

LAUNCH SITE: Launch at Garden Cove, just to the east of U.S. 1 where it is joined by Route 905 at the north end of Key Largo.

DIRECTIONS

Put in close to the Flamingo Restaurant at Garden Cove. Rattlesnake Key lies less than **half a mile** to the south, separated from Key Largo by North

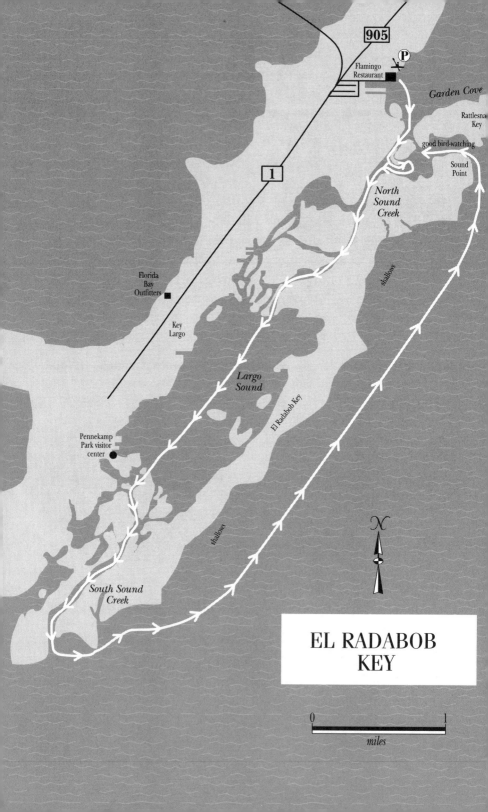

905

Flamingo
Restaurant

P

Garden Cove

Rattlesna[ke]
Key

good bird-watching

Sound
Point

1

North
Sound
Creek

shallows

Florida
Bay
Outfitters

Key
Largo

Largo
Sound

El Radabob Key

Pennekamp
Park visitor
center

shallows

South Sound
Creek

N

EL RADABOB
KEY

0   1

miles

Sound Creek. Enter the creek. The area immediately south, between Rattlesnake Key and El Radabob Key, is a good bird-watching area.

To the southwest, North Sound Creek branches into a series of narrow mangrove waterways. Explore to pick your own route to Largo Sound (generally southwest, **1.75 miles** or more along the creek depending on your chosen route).

Cross Large Sound for **1.5 miles** to the Pennekamp Park Visitor Center at the southwest corner of Largo Sound. John Pennekamp Coral Reef State Park (305–451–1202; www.penn-ekamp.com), which offers kayakers information about the reserve, was established in 1960 as America's first underwater park, at the time extending only 2 miles offshore. In a series of steps this led to the establishment in 1990 of the Florida Keys Sanctuary, which now extends from Biscayne National Park to the Dry Tortugas. The Visitor Center can be reached by kayak, or drive on Route 905, **4.75 miles** from the launch, following U.S. 1 toward Key West.

From the visitor center, paddle a **quarter mile** east to the navigation buoys that mark the entrance to South Sound Creek. Follow the markers through South Sound Creek for **1.6 miles** to the southern extremity of El Radabob Key, bringing you to the Atlantic coast.

For a sheltered return, retrace your path, exploring the different channels through the mangroves at both ends of Largo Sound.

Otherwise, continue to circle El Radabob Key as far as the northern end of Sound Point, at the first channel on your left (**4.8 miles**).

CAUTION: Maintain a distance of at least a quarter mile offshore to avoid shallows that will hinder your progress.

At Sound Point, turn left (west) through the sound south of Rattlesnake Key to North Sound Creek (**.7 mile**, 260 degrees) and follow the shore northward for **half a mile** to your put-in.

Where to Eat & Where to Stay

RESTAURANT *Flamingo Seafood Bar & Grill* (45 Garden Cove Drive, Key Largo; 305–451–8022) close by the put-in at Garden Cove, is worth checking out. Another option is *The Quay* restaurant, 2 miles south of Florida Bay Outfitters on the right side of U.S. 1. **LODGING** For accommodations and food at a friendly establishment managed by a sea kayaker, call Jamie Jackson (305–451–9968). Guests may launch their kayaks at his place, and a guide service is also offered.

Route 35:

---- --- ---- --- ---- ---- --- ---- -- →

Shell Key

This is a short round-trip to a mangrove island with a canopied tunnel and central lagoon. When you reach the northwest side of the island, look for the channel that leads into the center of the key. Natural tunnels lead beneath the canopy of mangrove; find the one that opens into the sheltered pool at the heart of the island. Approach quietly, as you are likely to find herons and anhingas and pelicans here.

TRIP HIGHLIGHTS: Attractive island with a lagoon enclosed by mangrove, within easy paddling range from shore.

TRIP RATING:
Basic

TRIP DURATION: 3 hours; 5 miles

NAVIGATION AIDS: Large-print Waterproof Charts #33E; NOAA chart #11449.

TIDAL INFORMATION: There is much shallow water in this area, and paddling will be easier around high tide. However, wading birds are more active at low water.

CAUTIONS: The boat channels in this area are the only routes for boats wishing to avoid the otherwise shallow water. Watch for powerboats, and keep to the side of the channels to avoid collision.

TRIP PLANNING: Take a marker, such as a baseball cap, to hang on the mangroves to indicate your exit point from the pool in the center of Shell Key.

LAUNCH SITE: Papa Joe's Marina, the launch site, is situated at the south end of Upper Matecumbe Key, on the northwest side of the road, at mile marker 79.7. Check in at the marina office for directions on launching and parking.

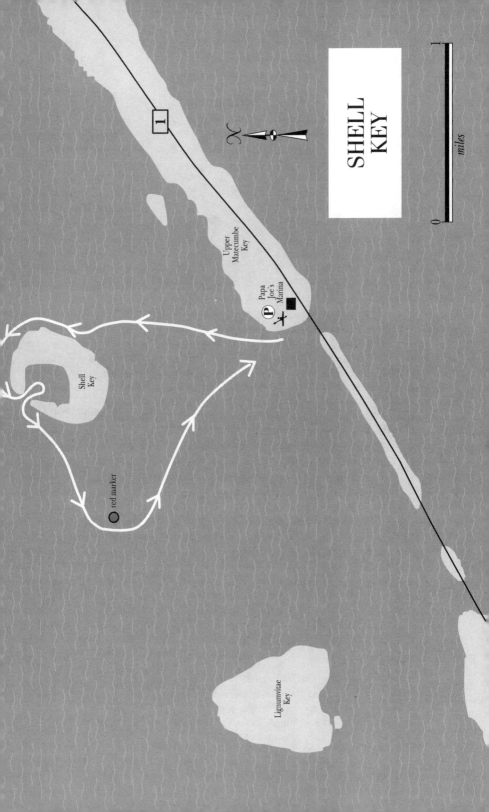

SHELL KEY

Upper
Matecumbe
Key

Papa
Joe's
Marina

Shell
Key

red marker

Lignumvitae
Key

miles

DIRECTIONS

From Papa Joe's, paddle north through Shell Key Channel. Aim toward the eastern end of Shell Key to keep in the deeper water (**1.5 miles**).

Circle Shell Key as far as the northwest side (**.5 mile**). Here, look for a channel beneath the canopy that leads to the pool in the center of the key. When you reach the pool, attach a marker to the mangrove to mark your exit point. (Don't forget to remove it when you leave.)

Out again from the mangroves, follow the shore of Shell Key to the westernmost point (**.4 mile**). You should now be able to see a red channel marker **1 mile** to the west, marking the entrance to a channel back to Papa Joe's. Cross to the red marker. The marina is almost **2 miles** from here, at a bearing of about 140 degrees.

Where to Eat & Where to Stay

RESTAURANT   Near the launch site at Papa Joe's is the upstairs *Tikki Bar*, plus a restaurant fronting the road. The Tikki Bar offers grilled sandwiches, black beans, and rice. The restaurant offers fish and Italian food.
LODGINGS   *The Kon Tiki*, about a mile north of Papa Joe's, is a small place with rooms on the bay and a tidal pool with fish (305–664–4702).
CAMPING   *Long Key State Recreation Area* has campsites by the Atlantic shore, some 10 miles south of Papa Joe's. Book well in advance for winter (305–664–4815). Another campsite is on Fiesta Key, 6 miles south of Papa Joe's.

Shell Key

Route 36:

━━ ━━ ━━ ━━ ━━ ━━ ━━ ━━ ━━ ━━ ━━ ➤

Lignumvitae Key

Lignumvitae Key has been owned by the state and the Nature Conservancy since 1970. It's the highest of all the keys at a spectacular 16 feet above sea level! In the nineteenth century, the key's giant mahogany trees were felled and in the 1920s some exotic plants and animals were introduced, but otherwise the tropical forest is considered to be virgin hammock, of a type once more widespread in Florida.

Tropical hardwood hammocks are considered to be the keystone habitat and the pinnacle of forest development on the Florida Keys. They are regarded as one of North America's rarest ecosystems.

Lignumvitae Key State Botanical Site has a significant area of remaining hammock. Most of the plants in a tropical hardwood hammock originate from the West Indies, carried in the storm winds or the crops of birds. Of more than 200 species of plants, trees, and shrubs that live there, thirty-six are listed as endangered or threatened.

Lignumvitae Key has one of the better preserved forests in Florida; there are still some 1,500 Lignumvitae trees there, making it one of the main places in the Florida Keys for this species of tree.

The Lignum vitae tree has an extremely dense, resin-rich timber, said to outlast bronze and steel as a boat-fitting material. Its hardness led to its common name "broke-iron tree." On Lignumvitae Key I'd recommend you land to take a guided tour of the forest.

See the Tarpon

Look down into the water at the end of the dock at Robbie's and you'll likely see huge tarpon. This is the result of a mercy mission by local fishermen who netted an injured tarpon years ago and brought it back to Robbie's. They kept it in a holding tank while a vet was brought to see if he could save the fish.

The tarpon survived and was released from the dock, but it remained in the vicinity, living off scraps thrown from the dock by fishermen.

This fish is long gone, but others attracted by the scraps and presumably feeling safe in the company of other tarpon, now gather here in a majestic shoal, outnumbering the pelicans that also gather in the hope of catching a snack.

TRIP HIGHLIGHTS: Tropical forest: mangrove channels on Matecumbe Key; the sight of tarpon swimming off the dock of Robbie's, a fishing charter and boat rental establishment, enrich this great trip.

TRIP RATING:
   Basic: An easy paddle.

TRIP DURATION: 2 to 3 hours; 4 to 5 miles. Add time to walk around Lignumvitae Key.

NAVIGATION AIDS: Large-print Waterproof Charts #33E; NOAA chart #11463.

TIDAL INFORMATION: This is an area of shallow water, but you can make the trip almost any time. Go at high water if you want more depth.

CAUTIONS: Most powerboat traffic is restricted by depth to the marked channels, but be watchful for boats.

TRIP PLANNING: This trip requires little planning, but if you have enough time, why not combine it with a trip to nearby Indian Key (Route 37)?

LAUNCH SITE: From the northeast end of Lower Matecumbe Key, cross the bridge (less than 1 mile) over Indian Key Channel.

Beyond the bridge are easy launching places to either side of the causeway, with parking close to the water.

Where to Eat & Where to Stay

RESTAURANTS Order fish at the little restaurant by Robbie's, by the bridge at the northeast end of Lower Matecumbe Key. The casual Lobster Walk at 74580 Overseas Highway (about 4 miles from your launch toward Key West) specializes in lobster and seafood (305–664–4399). **LODGING** Cottages and camping are available at *Fiesta Key Resort Campground* (800–562–7730). **CAMPING** *Long Key Recreation Area*, about 8 miles toward Key West, offers camping beside the ocean, but at a place where shallow water stretches far from shore (with a muddy clay bottom). Book early in winter (305–664–4815).

DIRECTIONS

Lignumvitae Key lies **1 mile** to the northwest, along Indian Key Channel. Keep to the edge of the channel to get deep water without obstructing the powerboat traffic. The landing place is easy to spot. Wait here for a guided tour, for which there is a $1.00 charge.

On your return, circle the island to the southwest corner (1 mile), then follow Lignumvitae Channel back to the northeast end of Lower Matecumbe Key (**1 mile**). There is an area of mangrove forest with narrow channels worth exploring on the northern end of Lower Matecumbe.

CAUTION: A clearly defined straight channel that passes through here is

Lignumvitae Key

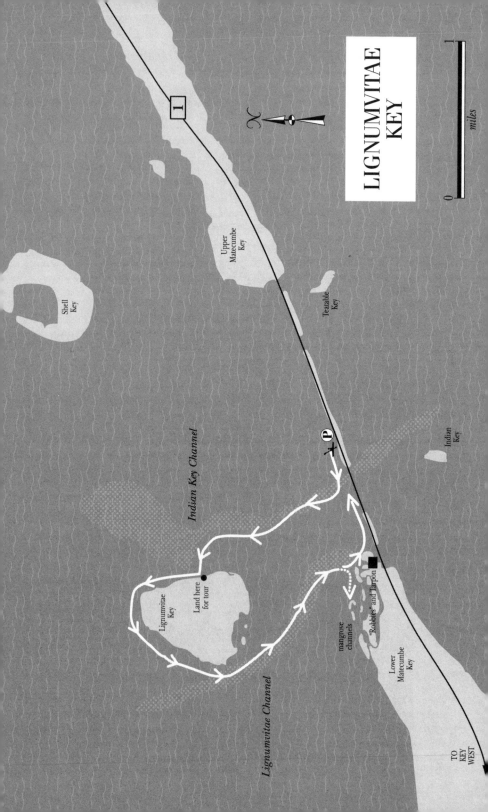

LIGNUMVITAE
KEY

miles

1

Shell
Key

Upper
Matecumbe
Key

Teatable
Key

Indian Key Channel

Land here
for tour

Lignumvitae
Key

Lignumvitae Channel

mangrove
channels

"Robbie's" and Tarpon

Lower
Matecumbe
Key

Indian
Key

TO
KEY
WEST

used as a shortcut by powerboats. Avoid this channel: It's a "prop channel," one in which the depth is sufficient for a boat to power through at planing speed, but too shallow for the hull at displacement speed. In short, if a boat slows down it will ground on the bottom and become stranded, so don't expect boats to reduce speed, even if you're in the way!

From the mangrove channels, return to Indian Key Channel. Where the bridge leaves Lower Matecumbe Key, you'll find a short dock and a restaurant, and Robbie's. From here, follow the bridge back to your launch site, (**1 mile**).

Route 37:

▬ ▬ ▬ ▬ ▬ ▬ ▬ ▬ ▬ ▬ ▬ ▬ ▬ ▬ ▬ ▬ ⟶

Indian Key

This is a short trip to an island where in 1840 some sixteen people were killed in a surprise Indian attack. At that time an entrepreneur named Houseman, who had already begun a number of profitable schemes on the island, was attempting to negotiate a permit from the government to hunt and kill Seminole Indians at $200 per head. A ranger-guided tour leads around the historic areas. You may contact the Indian Key State Historical Site at (305) 664–4815.

TRIP HIGHLIGHTS: A short and straightforward paddle with a tour of a historic island.

TRIP RATING:
   Basic: An easy trip.

TRIP DURATION: 2 to 3 hours; 1.5 miles.

NAVIGATION AIDS: Large-print Waterproof Charts #33E.

TIDAL INFORMATION: Mudflats appear between the island and the causeway at low water.

TRIP PLANNING: A trip around high tide when the mudflats are covered will give a more open feel and is more likely to offer the legendary Florida Keys water colors of blue and green. Take bug repellent for the island tour.

LAUNCH SITE: Launch from the U.S. 1 causeway that runs between Lower and Upper Matecumbe Keys, at a point about 1 mile northeast of Lower Matecumbe Key, in the vicinity of Indian Key Channel. There are numerous good places to launch from the beaches on the southeast side of the road.

Lightning

We paddled in heat. A baseball cap and sunglasses cut the glare, but the oppressive humidity of Florida in August caught our throats. Above the Atlantic, bubbling cauliflower clouds blanket the sky.

"It's getting a bit close, that one, Nigel," said my friend, Kevin, a helicopter pilot. "We follow a five-mile rule out on the airfield. Any closer and we get the hell out of there!"

I watched the cloud. A streak of white trembled for a moment against the oppressive gray. Another silver streak. I counted ten seconds between the flash and the rumble, but I couldn't remember the rule of thumb for calculating how far we were from the strike. I was visiting from Britain, and hadn't experienced many thunderstorms.

"Let's get off the water," Kevin said urgently. "It's headed this way!"

We retreated fast. Suddenly the sky glared brilliant for several staggering moments and the roar exploded with it. We sprinted for the cover of the buildings, deserting the kayaks on the sand.

The storm was overhead. Rain sheeted down. Water rushed across the parking lot and poured from flooded gutters. The sky sparked, fizzed, and rumbled.

I wondered how great the risk is of being struck by lightning. Palm Beach Weather Department spokesman Paul Houle informed me that on average, ninety-three deaths and three hundred injuries are caused by lightning strikes every year in the United States. It has been reported that activity around the water accounts for 40 percent of the deaths, and that more canoeists die of lightning strikes than of any other cause. Houle said that the weather department counted ten thousand individual strikes from a single Florida storm. Florida is a hot spot for thunderstorms, especially in summer.

And concerning that important rule of thumb: Count the seconds from the lightning flash until the sound reaches you and divide by five to discover how far the strike was away from you in miles. Less than five miles (25 seconds) and you should be off the water. For more tips on thunderstorm safety, see the introduction to this book.

From your launching place make your way to Indian Key Channel. Indian Key lies just **half a mile** to the south.

Paddle directly to the island, keeping to the deeper water where necessary, and pull ashore at the landing.

Return to the causeway after your tour of the island.

Where to Eat & Where to Stay

RESTAURANTS There is a fish bar beside Robbie's (mile marker 84.5) and a kayak rental company on the northwest side of U.S. 1. At mile marker 81.6 to the south is the *Islamorada Fish Company*, which began as a wholesale fish market and now serves lunch and dinner, with basket meals outside. It's on the bay side, so good for sunsets (305–664–9271). **LODGING** Cottages and camping are available at *Fiesta Key Resort campground* (800–562–7730). **CAMPING** *Long Key State Recreation Area* offers camping beside the ocean (305–664–4815). It is on Long Key, 9 miles toward Key West on U.S. 1, between 9 and 12 miles from your launch site.

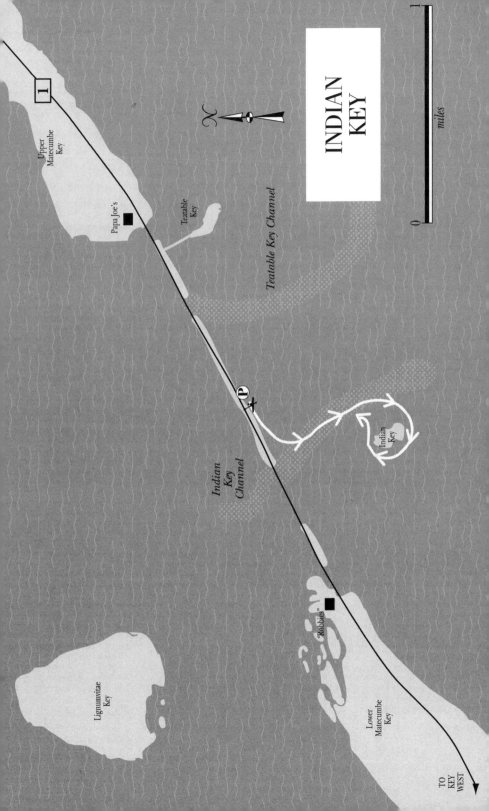

INDIAN KEY

miles

0 ... 1

Upper
Matecumbe
Key

1

Papa Joe's ■

Teatable
Key

Teatable Key Channel

P

Indian
Key

Indian
Key
Channel

Lignumvitae
Key

"Robbies" ■

Lower
Matecumbe
Key

TO
KEY
WEST

Route 38:

Raccoon Key

Begin this elliptical route from a ramp on Cudjoe Key close by the land mooring site for the gigantic white observation blimps that are reeled out on long cables to float in the air above the Florida Keys. Supposedly they keep a watchful eye on drug traffickers and boat movements in the region—but who knows what they really do up there? There are normally two, one in the air and a spare down on land. The first blimp in service was affectionately known as Fat Albert.

Our route follows the stepping stones of the Little Swash Keys and the Tarpon Belly Keys to Raccoon Key. Raccoon Key is home to a colony of rhesus monkeys, bred for research purposes. The shallow waters close to Raccoon Key are sheltered grounds favored by small sharks and barracuda. I recommend a circuit of Raccoon Key, both to watch the fish and to see the monkeys inside the fence.

The stepping-stone nature of this trip continues with the homeward journey via Hurricane Key and the three Budd Keys, which offer good shelter from wind. A number of crossings are involved, but none longer than about a mile.

TRIP HIGHLIGHTS: Sea wildlife and rhesus monkeys.
TRIP RATING:
    Basic/intermediate: A good trip!
TRIP DURATION: Half day to full day; 8.2 miles.
NAVIGATION AIDS: Waterproof Charts #34E; NOAA chart #11445.

Rhesus Monkeys

Raccoon Key and Lois Key on the Atlantic side of Florida differ from the other keys in that they are populated by rhesus monkeys. My friends told me they were huge and ferocious and were reputed to drag passing fishermen from their boats, so I was both curious and apprehensive about paddling out to Raccoon Key. The monkeys do look large and somewhat intimidating from a distance, so the fences and NO LANDING signs around the coast are superfluous. The mangroves provide good conditions in which the monkeys can live and breed, so there is no need for a live-in caretaker. The monkeys don't like to go into the water, so they don't escape, and the island is uninhabited by people.

Rhesus monkeys have for a long time been used as laboratory animals because of their similarity to man, with many of the animals initially being imported from India. When India banned their export in 1977, breeding programs, such as the ones on the two keys, were developed to maintain a supply for the U.S. Food and Drug Administration.

Recently the state started proceedings to have the monkeys removed on grounds of pollution, so perhaps the unusual attraction of seeing monkeys on a Florida paddling trip will disappear in the future. Go see them while you still can.

TIDAL INFORMATION: Insignificant tide.

TRIP PLANNING: There is a shortage of landing options if you heed the NO TRESPASSING signs. Be prepared to stop on the water for a lunch break. However, the water is less than 2 feet deep throughout most of this area. Wear foot protection in case you wish to stand; there are sting rays. Raccoon Key offers superb opportunities for watching sharks and other fish in shallow water, so I recommend polarized sunglasses so you can see them better.

LAUNCH SITE: On Cudjoe Key, look for Mick's Auto and Marine. The turn north onto Blimp Road is close by, but is not marked on all road maps. The turn is close to a slight bend in U.S. 1. Blimp

Road runs almost due north to the coast, ending at a public boat ramp. Parking is free, but after unloading, please park back from the shore to leave room for people to maneuver boat trailers.

DIRECTIONS

Launch from the boat ramp and turn left (northwest) past the blimps.

When you reach the northwest corner of Cudjoe Key, (**.5 mile**), cross to the small group of mangrove clumps, the Little Swash Keys (**.5 mile**).

Roughly to the north from these you will see the Tarpon Belly Keys. The crossing to these keys is about **1 mile**.

Now paddle northeast for about **1 mile** from Tarpon Belly Keys to Raccoon Key.

Circle Raccoon Key a distance of **2.4 miles**.

From the western side of Raccoon Key, start your return trip by paddling south to Hurricane Key (**.5 mile**).

From Hurricane Key, continue almost south to the northernmost Budd Key (**.5 mile**). From here, continue south but paddle via each of the other Budd Keys back to Cudjoe Key (**1.5 miles**).

NOTE: If you pass to the east of the two more westerly Budd Keys, the blimp on the ground, if there is one, will be hidden from sight until you round the southern tip of the southernmost island—but you will still be able to see the top of the pylon that indicates its position.

Where to Eat & Where to Stay

RESTAURANTS   At about mile marker 20 on U.S. 1 on Cudjoe Key is a restaurant called **Mangrove Mama's** (305–745–3030), which serves seafood, hamburgers, and the like. Not high dining, but on the good side. **Baby's Coffee Roasters** is at mile marker 15 on U.S. 1—a cafe that not surprisingly features coffee. On weekends at the cafe, there is the addition of the **Smokehouse Restaurant**, which serves great barbecue-style meals for eating inside or out (305–744–0128). **LODGING AND CAMPING** **Bahia Honda State Park** on Bahia Honda Key, about 13 miles north on I–5 from Cudjoe Key, offers camping and self-catering cabins (maximum six persons per cabin). This is the southernmost and busiest state park. Book well in advance (306–872–2353).

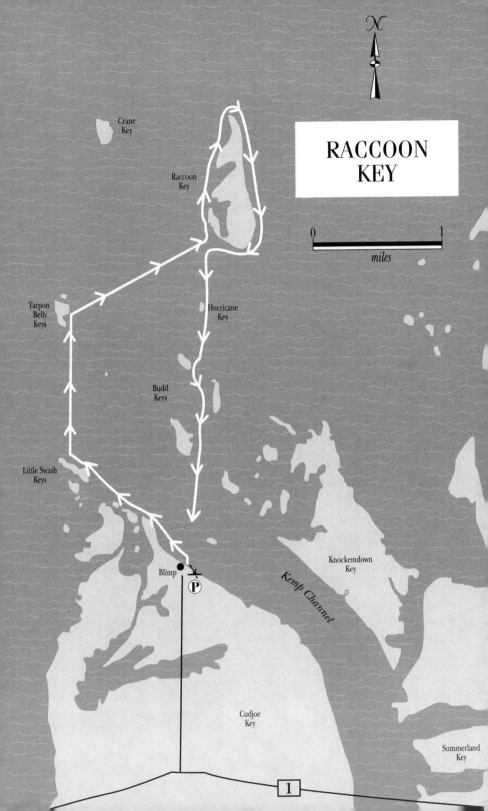

The Sharks of Raccoon Key

A circuit of Raccoon Key, hugging the shore, will reveal shoals of fish cruising in the clear, shallow water over crusts of coral. Look for the sandy brown nurse sharks, recognizable by two dorsal fins and a squat shape. Look also for the streamlined black-tipped shark, with black at the uppermost tip of its tail fin. We also spotted rays, and many small barracuda. The most sheltered water offers the best view of the fish and sharks. They're easiest to see among the mangroves, where the coral is close to the surface.

Mosquitoes Foil Bats

At the end of a small road on Sugarloaf Key, next to Cudjoe Key, is a muddy area with a strange-looking tower. It was built to house bats. The man responsible was a perky Florida real estate salesman who bought Sugarloaf Key early this century with the idea of building a resort town and becoming rich. His plans were foiled by the severity of the mosquito problem.

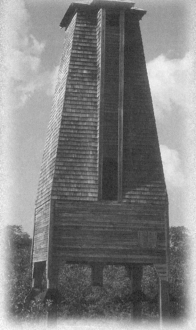

When this fellow heard that bats eat enormous numbers of mosquitoes, he invested in a bat tower and a specially formulated compound to attract bats to settle there.

Like his plan to draw tourists to the island, his plan to attract bats failed, and the man went bankrupt. The shingled tower still remains. It now serves as a perfect roosting place for mosquitoes.

Route 39:

━ ▰ ▰ ━ ▰ ▰ ━ ▰ ▰ ━ ▰ ▰ ━ ▰ ━ ▰ ▰ ━ ━➤

Geiger Key

Aleisurely circuit of Geiger Key offers shelter and shallow water, so it makes a great beginner trip. You stand a good chance of seeing a lot of birds in the "lake" section to the north of Geiger Key, as well as fish to the south. There are lots of opportunities for rest stops.

TRIP HIGHLIGHTS: Watching the fish over the coral heads, and the birds north of the key.

TRIP RATING:
Basic: Suitable for beginners.

TRIP DURATION: 4 hours; 4 miles.

NAVIGATION AIDS: Large-print Waterproof Charts #34E; NOAA chart #11445.

TIDAL INFORMATION: Much of this trip is in shallow water. Paddling will be easier if you are afloat through the highest part of the tide.

TRIP PLANNING: For watching fish, take polarized sunglasses, or use a face mask and lean across another kayak to dip your face into the water.

LAUNCH SITE: On Big Coppitt Key going east, take a right turn onto Boca Chica Road. In 1.2 miles, now on Geiger Key, take the left turn just before the bend in the road. This is Geiger Road, entry to Geiger Key Marina and a launching place (fee). But almost immediately next door is a fenced enclosure where you can park and a small beach from which you can launch, both free. This area is maintained by the Navy.

DIRECTIONS

Looking out from the beach toward the southwest, through the gap between Saddlehill Key and Geiger Key, you'll see markers out in the water—two in the middle of the gap and another pair to the left just beyond the mangroves. This left pair warn of rocks. Paddle **a quarter mile** to this area. The water is shallow here, with coral heads and an amazing variety of fish.

Cross to the southwest for **half a mile** from here to the obvious point of Geiger Key. Then follow the shore and the bay beyond for **half a mile** to the entrance to Geiger Creek.

Follow the creek under the bridge and inland for **three-quarters of a mile** until you reach a shallow saltwater "lake."

Explore this pool at your leisure. It is shallow throughout, which discourages hurrying. It also attracts birds and makes this an excellent place for watching waders. The direct distance across the pool is **1.4 miles**.

Exit the pool at the eastern shore where the road crosses. This brings you into Similar Sound. Turn right (south) and follow the shore for **three-quarters of a mile** to finish at your original launching place.

Where to Eat & Where to Stay

RESTAURANTS   You can get a drink and something to eat at *Geiger Key Marina*, adjacent to your launch. Otherwise it's worth taking a short drive into Key West for a choice of restaurants, including *the Half Shell Raw Bar*, which overlooks the water in Lands End Village, Key West (305–294–7496) for fresh seafood. **LODGINGS AND CAMPING**   Nearby Key West has a plethora of options. Call visitors information at (305) 294–4265 or call the chamber of commerce at (305) 294–2587 for suggestions and directions.

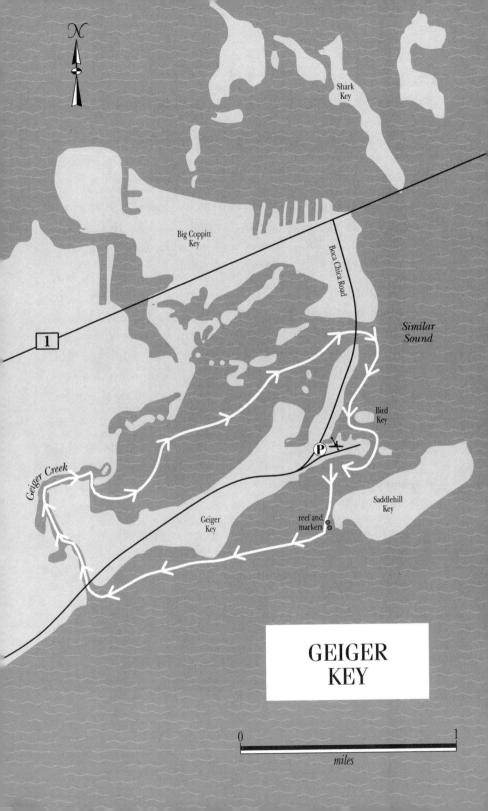

N

1

Shark
Key

Big Coppitt
Key

Boca Chica Road

Similar
Sound

Bird
Key

P

Geiger Creek

Geiger
Key

reef and
markers

Saddlehill
Key

GEIGER
KEY

0   1
miles

Route 40:

Snipe Point and the Mud Keys

U.S. 1 links the largest of the Lower Keys, which string together to make up the Atlantic coast of the Florida Keys. A string of smaller barrier islands, running roughly parallel to the highway and about 5 miles to the north, makes up the Gulf of Mexico coastline.

The paddling route for this trip circles out to these barrier islands, extending beyond Snipe Key and the Mud Keys onto the open Gulf before returning via a stepping-stone route to the start. The waters between the Atlantic and the Gulf keys is shallow, and this whole journey can be completed without paddling over water more than 3 or 4 feet deep. In theory you could walk it!

Be sure to take polarized sunglasses so you get a good view of the fish, sponges, and jellyfish beneath you, or a mask so you can hold onto another kayak for support as you dip your face into the warm water for an even better view.

The mangrove islands on this route are roosting places for herons, egrets, and pelicans, and the outer islands have sandy beaches and offshore coral heads in water clear as glass. Watch for egrets and ibis flocking to their roosting grounds in the evening.

TRIP HIGHLIGHTS: Shallow seas that offer an opportunity to view a delightful range of sea creatures such as rays, sharks, and sponges.

TRIP RATING:
> *Advanced:* Requires sustained vigorous paddling, although the paddling is fairly straightforward.

TRIP DURATION: Full day; 17.35 miles.

NAVIGATION AIDS: Waterproof Charts #34; NOAA chart #11445.

TIDAL INFORMATION: No significant tides.

CAUTIONS: The near-impenetrable mangroves make landing almost impossible on most islands along the route. Although the water is shallow enough to stand almost anywhere along the way, the rich seabed life of upside-down jellyfish and sponges, and fish including sting rays, sharks, and barracuda, might persuade you to wait until you reach Snipe Point. If you do wade, wear shoes.

TRIP PLANNING: Make sure you carry drink and food. The area is full of mangrove islands and it is essential you take a chart and compass to align yourself correctly.

LAUNCH SITE: There are two boat ramps at the eastern end of Big Coppitt Key, where U.S. 1 crosses Similar Sound, on the south side of the road. Find parking nearby.

DIRECTIONS

Launch into Similar Sound and paddle **half a mile** roughly northeast to pass under the U.S. 1 bridge. The key to your left is Shark Key. The one to the north is O'Hara Key.

Follow the shore of Shark Key until O'Hara Key no longer blocks your view to the north, about a **quarter mile**.

From here, follow a northerly bearing for **3.5 miles** to the middle Snipe Key. On your way you will pass close to the east of Round Key, to the west of the Crane Keys, and to the east of Waltz Key. Make slight diversions to visit these keys, each of which is a beautiful tangle of mangrove used by roosting and nesting birds.

Follow the mangrove shore of the middle Snipe Key to the northwestern tip, about **three-quarters of a mile**. Then cross to the next of the Snipe Keys, a couple of hundred yards to the north. Keep to the east of this key and continue north for **1 mile**, keeping the Snipe Keys to your left.

Snipe Point and the Mud Keys

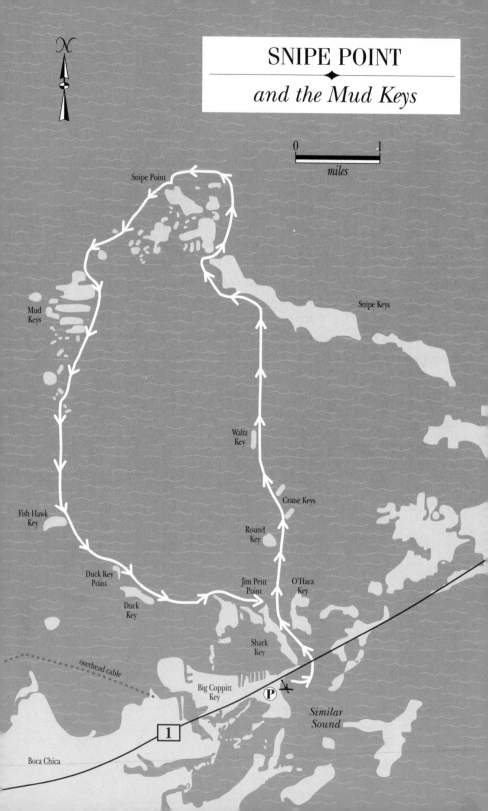

CAUTION: There is shallow water here, so you may need to paddle farther east, especially at low water.

When you reach the open water of the Gulf of Mexico, Snipe Point will lie just over **half a mile** to the west.

You'll find fine sandy beaches at Snipe Point, especially at low tide. There has been land on this Snipe Key for a sufficient time for the progression of vegetation to include less salt-tolerant species of trees. Here's a good place for a lunch stop and a walk to stretch your legs.

From Snipe Point, the Mud Keys lie about **1.5 miles** to the southwest. If you take a seaward route to the Mud Keys, watch for coral heads beneath you, where you may see a lot of attractive fish.

The Mud Keys extend about **1.5 miles** to the south and are crossed by many channels, making this a great area to explore.

From the southernmost Mud Keys, cross **1.5 miles** to Fish Hawk Key. (From Fish Hawk Key, you should be able to see overhead cables **1.5 miles** to the south, confirming your position.)

Cross from Fish Hawk Key to Duck Key Point, (**.75 mile**, 130 degrees) and continue to the southeast end of Duck Key (**.75 mile**).

Cross to Jim Pent Point (**.75 miles east**), then a further **half mile** to the northern tip of Shark Key.

Now reverse your outward route, following the shore of Shark Key southeast (watch for the shallows) back to the bridge and around to your original put-in, about **1.25 miles**.

Snipe Point and the Mud Keys

Stingray Tale

By Michael Gray

Paddling in the warm shallow waters of Southern Florida affords both a view above the water and below its dancing surface. But the animal life that inhabits these gin-clear waters can be so well disguised that you often don't see it until it suddenly flees from the huge predator that it thinks you are. Even a five-foot stingray can vanish from sight as wave action covers its back with sand.

I was cruising along in 8 inches of water of such clarity it felt as though I was suspended above patchy vegetation, sponges, and patches of sand. Suddenly the seabed appeared to buckle underneath me! Water erupted from either side, swamping the cockpit, and my kayak ran aground.

Then my bow lifted from the water on the back of a massive stingray as it flapped its great wings. The ray flew with such power that it skated across the water for about 20 yards, carrying me with it, before it found deep enough water to dive and swim away.

Where to Eat & Where to Stay

RESTAURANTS   Visit *Pepe's* at 806 Caroline Street, Key West (305–294–7192). On the wall is a photo of a kayak being paddled down the street. My friend Bill tells me Pepe's used to display a blue neon sign on the front door saying "closed," while locals entered by the side door. The food is good and fresh.
LODGING   There are lodgings and restaurants galore in Key West; after all, it is a holiday resort. There are plenty of bars, too. For an entertaining and informative guide to Key West lodgings and restaurants, dip into the Key West section of *The Florida Keys*, by Joy Williams. Alternatively the chamber of commerce (305–294–2587) or the visitors information center (305–294–4265) should have some suggestions.

Appendix A

Paddlesports Rentals, Tours, Sales, Instruction, and Shuttle

Note: Codes follow each establishment to indicate some of the services provided—paddlesports rentals (R), tours (T), sales (S), instruction (I), accommodation (A), and shuttle (SH).

Rentals may offer sea kayaks sit-on-tops, touring kayaks, or canoes. For some of the listings below, mailing addresses are given instead of street addresses. Please call establishments for directions in these instances.

Adventure Sea Kayak, Captiva Island, FL; (941) 437–0956. (T,I)

Adventure Times Kayaks, three locations: Downtown West Palm Beach, Riviera Beach Marina, and 521 Northlake Boulevard, North Palm Beach, FL 33408; (561) 881–7218. (R, T, S, I)

Atlantic Coast Kayak Corporation, 1869 South Dixie Highway, Pompano Beach (Miami area), FL 33060-8948; (954) 781–0073. (R, T, S, I)

Baby's Kayak Works, 3200 U.S. 1 (mile marker 15), Key West, FL 33040; (305) 744–0128. (R, T)

Bahia Honda State Park Concession, 36850 Overseas Highway, Big Pine Key, FL 33043 (mailing address); located on U.S. 1 MM 37, Bahia Honda Key; (305) 872–3210. (R)

Bill Jackson's Inc., 9501 U.S. 19 North, Pinellas Park, St. Petersburg, FL 34616; (813) 576–4196. (R, T, S, I)

By the Bay Outfitters, 520 Blackburn Point Road, Osprey, FL 34229; (941) 966–3937. (R, T, S)

Canoe Country Outfitters, 6493 54th Avenue North, St. Petersburg, FL 33709; (813) 545–4554. (R, S)

Canoe Outfitters of Florida, 8900 West Indiantown Road, Jupiter, FL 33478; (561) 746–7053. (R, T)

Canoe Outpost, Little Manatee River, 18001 U.S. Highway 301 South, Wimauma, FL 33598; (813) 634–2228 or (800) 229–1371. (R, I, T)

Canoe Outpost, Peace River, 2816 N.W. County Road 661, Arcadia, FL 34266; located one mile west of Arcadia, next door to Peace River Campground off Highway 70 West; (941) 494–1215 or (800) 268–0083.(R)

Canoe Safari, 3020 N.W. County Road 661, Arcadia, FL 34266; (941) 494–7863 or (800) 262–1119. (R)

Cayo Caribe Kayaks, 1018 Truman Avenue, Key West, FL 33040; (305) 296–4115. (T)

Cedar Bay Marina, 705 Elkcam Circle, Marco Island, FL 34145-2553; (941) 394–9333.

Estero River Outfitters, 20991 South Tamiami Trail, Estero, FL 33928; (941) 992–4050. (R, T, S, I)

Flamingo Lodge, Marina and Outpost Resort, Flamingo, FL 33030; (800) 600–3813 or (941) 695–3101. (R)

Florida Bay Outfitters, 104050 Overseas Highway, Key Largo, FL 33037; (305) 451–3018. (R, T, I, S, SH)

Florida Keys Kayaking, MM 77.5 Overseas Highway, Islamorada, FL 33036; (305) 664–4424. (R, T, I)

Get Wet Sports, 203 Capri Boulevard, Naples, FL 34113; (941) 394–9557. (R, T)

Grande Tours, P.O. Box 281, 11 Fishery Road, Placida, FL 33946–0281; (941) 697–8825. (T, R, SH—across-water)

Gulf Coast Kayaks, Bokeelia, Pine Island, FL 33922; (941) 283–1125. (R, T, SH)

Island Kayak, 201 William Street, Key West, FL 33040-6679; (305) 292–0059. (R, T, SH)

J. Jackson, 221 West Canal Drive, Key Largo, FL 33037; (305) 451–9968. (T, I, A)

Jig's Bait and Tackle, P.O. Box 431752, Big Pine Key, FL 33043 (mailing address); located at MM 82.5 on U.S. 1; (305) 872–1040. (R, T, SH)

Kayak Treks, 1239 Beneva Road South, Sarasota, FL 34232; (941) 365–3892 or (800) 656–3891. (T)

Keys Wind 'n' Sport, P.O. Box 2016, Islamorada, FL 33036 (mailing address); located at MM 82.5 on U.S. 1, (305) 664–4830. (R, T, S, I)

Suncoast Sea Kayaks
Canoe Country Outfitters
Bill Jackson's
Sweetwater Kayaks

Canoe Outpost Little Manatee River
Ray's Canoe Hideaway

Myakka Outpost

Silent Sports
Kayak Treks
Outdoor Products Store   Canoe   Canoe Outpost, Peace River   Peace River Canoes
By the Bay Outfitters   Safari   Canoe Safari   Canoe Outfitters of Florida
                                                     Southern Exposure Sea Kayaks
Snook Haven Retreat   Adventure Times

Grande Tours Placida

Lee County Manatee Park
Gulf Coast Kayaking

Adventure Sea Kayaks   Nautical Ventures
Tarpon Bay, Rentals and Tours
Wild Vision
Estero River Outfitters

Naples Sea Kayaking Adventures
Get Wet Sports
Cedar Bay Marina
Marco River Marina

                                        Atlantic Coast Kayak Co.
                                        Urban Trails Kayaks
North American Canoe Tours   Waterways Kayaks

                                        Florida Bay Outfitters
                                        J. Jackson
                  Flamingo Lodge

PADDLING OUTFITTERS
♦
*Paddlesports rentals, sales,
shuttle & instruction*

                              Keys Wind 'n' Sport
                              Papa Joe's Marina
                              Sail 'n' Yak Center
                              Florida Keys Kayaking

          Bahia Honda
          State Park
Cayo Caribe Kayaks   Lost World Adventures
Mosquito Coast Island Outfitters   Jig's Bait and Tackle
Island Kayak   Baby's Kayak Works

N

Lee County Manatee Park, 1.5 miles east of I–75 exit 25; (941) 432–2004. 10901 State Road 80, Fort Myers, FL 33905.

Lost World Adventures, P.O. Box 431311, 319 Lucretia Street, Big Pine Key, FL 33043; (305) 872–1040. (R, T, SH)

Marco River Marina, Marco Island, FL 34145-2399; (941) 389–0393. (R)

Mosquito Coast Island Outfitters, 1107 Duval Street, Key West, FL 33040; (305) 294–7178. (T)

Myakka Outpost, Inc., 13207 State Road 72, Sarasota, FL 34241; (941) 923–1120. (R)

Naples Sea Kayaking Adventures, 360 25th Avenue S.W., Naples, FL, 34117; (941) 353–4878. (T, I, SH)

Nautical Ventures, 750 East Pompano Beach, FL 33064; (305) 667–2969. (S)

North American Canoe Tours, Everglades Outpost, P.O. Box 5038, 107 Camellia Street, Everglades City, FL 34139; (941) 695–4666 (winter), (860) 739–0791 (summer). (R, T, SH—by land or water)

Outdoor Products Store, 5341 Fruitville Road, Sarasota, FL 34232; (941) 371–4677. (S)

Papa Joe's Marina, P.O. Box 464, 79700 Overseas Highway, Islamorada, Florida Keys, FL 33036 (mailing address); on U.S. 1, MM 79.7, Upper Matecumbe Key; (305) 664–5005. (R)

Peace River Canoes Inc., 2184 East Main Street, Wauchula, FL 33873; (941) 773–6370. (R)

Ray's Canoe Hideaway, 1247 Haggle Park Road, Bradenton, FL 34302; (941) 747–3909. (R, T)

Sail 'n' Yak Center, at Hampton Inn and Suites, 80001 Overseas Highway, Islamorada, FL 33036; (305) 664–3505. (R, T,)

Silent Sports of Florida, Southpointe Mall/Marina, 7660 South Tamiami Trail, U.S. 41, Sarasota, FL 34241; (941) 922–4042. (R, S, T)

Snook Haven Retreat, 500 East Venice, Venice, FL 34292; (941) 485–7221. (R)

Southern Exposure Sea Kayaks, P.O. Box 4530, Tequesta, FL 33469 (mailing address); located at 18487 S.E. Federal Highway, Blowing Rocks Marina, U.S. 1, 1 mile north from Jupiter Inlet; (561) 575–4530. Rental fees go directly to a Loxahatchee River fund. (R, S, I)

Suncoast Sea Kayaks, 10900 Oakhurst Road, Largo, FL 33774; (813) 595–3220. (S)

Sweetwater Kayaks Outfitters St. Petersburg, 1136 Pinellas Bayway, Tierra Verde, FL 33715; (727) 906–0708. (R, S, I, SH)

Tarpon Bay Rentals and Tours, 900 Tarpon Bay Road, Sanibel Island, FL 33957; (941) 472–8900. (R, T)

Urban Trails Kayaks, 10800 Collins Avenue, Miami, FL 33154; (305) 947–1302. (R, T, S)

Waterways Kayaks, on the Intracoastal Highway, behind the Westlake Wildlife Refuge, 1406 North Ocean Drive, Hollywood, FL 33019; (954) 921–8944. (R, S, I)

Wild Vision, Lovers Key State Park, 8700 Estero Boulevard, Fort Myers Beach, FL 33931. (R, T, S, I, SH)

Appendix B

State Parks, Museums and Reserves

Note: For some of the listings below, mailing addresses are given instead of street addresses. Please call for directions in these instances.

Bahia Honda State Park, 3685 Overseas Highway, Big Pine Key, FL 33043; (305) 872–2353.

Biscayne Aqua Center, Biscayne National Park, 9700 S.W. 328th Street, Homestead, FL 33033-5635; (305) 247–2400. Canoe rentals.

Cayo Costa State Park, c/o Barrier Islands GEOpark, P.O. Box 1150 Boca Grande, FL 33921; (941) 964–0375.

Center for Marine Conservation (Florida Keys office), 513 Fleming Street, Suite 14, Key West, FL 33040; (305) 295–3370.

Delnor–Wiggins Pass State Recreation Area, 11100 Gulfshore Drive North, Naples, FL 33963; (941) 597–6196.

Egmont Key State Park, Slip 656–4275, 34th Street South, St. Petersburg, FL 33711; (813) 893–2627.

Everglades National Park, 40001 State Road 9336, Homestead, FL 33034–6733; (305) 242–7700.

Egmont Key
State Park

Myakka River
State Park

Mote Marine Lab
Pelican Man's Bird Sanctuary
Selby Botanical Gardens
Spanish Point Mounds

Gasparilla Island
State Recreation Area

Cayo Costa
State Park

J. N. Ding Darling
National Wildlife
Reserve

Delnor-Wiggins Pass
State Recreation Area

Smallwood
Store Museum

Lee County
Manatee Park

Lover's Key State
Recreation Area

Everglades
National
Park

Jonathan
Dickinson
State Park
Florida
History Center
and Museum

Biscayne
Aqua Center

John Pennekamp
Coral Reef
State Park

N

STATE PARKS,
◆
MUSEUMS, AND RESERVES

Lignumvitae
Key State Botanical
Site

Indian Key
State Historic Site

Long Key
State Recreation Area

Center for
Marine
Conservation

Bahia Honda
State Park

Florida History Center and Museum, 805 North U.S. 1, Jupiter, FL 33477; (561) 747–6639. Always features displays about local history and natural history, plus a changing display of a topical subject.

Florida Marine Patrol Emergency Number, (800) 342–5367 or (800) DIAL–FMP.

Florida Professional Paddlesports Association, P.O. Box 1764, Arcadia, FL 34265.

Gasparilla Island State Recreation Area, c/o Barrier Islands GEOpark, P.O. Box 1150, Boca Grande, FL 33921; (941) 964–0375.

Indian Key State Historic Site, c/o Lignumvitae Key State Botanical Site, P.O. Box 1052, Islamorada, FL 33036; (305) 664–4815.

J. N. "Ding" Darling National Wildlife Refuge, 1 Wildlife Drive, Sanibel, FL 33957; (941) 472–1100. Offers a visitors center, wildlife drive, walking trails, and the opportunity to see and identify birds such as herons, egrets, and ospreys, and to view alligators.

John Pennekamp Coral Reef State Park, P.O. Box 487, Key Largo, FL 33037; (305) 451–1202.

Jonathan Dickinson State Park, 16450 S.E. Federal Highway, Hobe Sound, FL 33455; (561) 546–2771.

Lignumvitae Key State Botanical Site, P.O. Box 1052, Islamorada, FL 33036; (305) 664–4815. Features tropical hardwood hammock.

Lee County Manatee Park, 10901 State Road 80, Fort Myers, FL 33905; (941) 432–2004. Manatee viewing update line: (941) 694–3537. Features walkways and viewing platforms overlooking a warm water channel where manatees gather.

Long Key State Recreation Area, P.O. Box 776, Overseas Highway, Long Key, FL 33001; (305) 664–4815.

Lovers Key State Recreation Area, 8700 Estero Boulevard, Fort Myers Beach, FL 33931; (941) 463–4588.

Mote Marine Laboratory, 1600 Ken Thompson Parkway, Sarasota, FL 34236. A good place to learn about local species of marine life, this nonprofit independent research laboratory displays more than 200 varieties of Florida marine life, some inside a 135,000 gallon shark tank with side view. A second site, the Mote Marine sea turtle program (941–388–4331), houses sea turtles and manatees.

Myakka River State Park, 13207 State Road 72, Sarasota, FL 34241; (941) 361–6511.

National Marine Sanctuary Program, 5550 Overseas Highway, Marathon, FL 33050; (305) 292–0311. Manages marine areas of special national significance, and offers information about areas with restricted or prohibited access within the National Marine Sanctuary.

Pelican Man's Bird Sanctuary, 1708 Ken Thompson Parkway, Sarasota, FL 34236; (941) 388–4444. Cares for injured birds and is operated by more than 230 volunteers under the guidance of Pelican Man, Dale Shields. You'll see many of the local and migratory species here, so it's a great way to become familiar with the identification of Florida birds. Free admission.

Selby Botanical Gardens, 811 South Palm Avenue, Sarasota, FL 34236-7726; (941) 366–5730. Eleven acres of grounds and glass houses housing a collection of 20,000 plants. An excellent place to get to grips with the identification of Florida plants, although the orchid collection here steals the show. Specializes in botanical research, plant identification, and micropropagaton. Adult admission fee is $6.00.

Smallwood Store Museum, P.O. Box 367, Chokoloskee, FL 34138; to get here, cross the causeway to Chokoloskee. The museum is at the end of the first street on the right; (941) 695–2989. A historic outpost store.

Spanish Point Mounds, 500 North Tamiami Trail U.S. 41, Osprey, FL 34229; (941) 966–5214. A thirty acre preserve close to Osprey, South Sarasota, encloses prehistoric Indian mounds from 2150 B.C. Possibly the best interpretive center for an Indian site in southwest Florida.

Appendix C

Some Local Events

Ocean Challenge, first weekend in May, canoe and kayak race, Westin Resort Miami Beach; (305) 932–3979.

Indian Key Festival kayak race, early October. Write Friends of Islamorada Area State Parks, P.O. Box 236, Islamorada, FL 33036–0236; (305) 451–3018.

Backwater Nick's canoe and kayak races, around February 21; fax (941) 642–6667.

Sea Kayaking Symposium, last weekend of each February. Contact Sweetwater Kayaks Outfitters, 1136 Pinellas Bayway, Tierra Verde, FL 33715; (727) 906–0708.

Captiva Challenge, first weekend in December. Includes tours and races on Captiva Island. Contact Trade Association of Paddle Sports, 1245 North Wauwatosa Road, Mequon WI 53097; (888) 732–8275.

Appendix D

Paddling Clubs

Coconut Kayakers, P.O. Box 3646, Tequesta, FL 33469.

Central Florida Paddling Masters, 2460 Avenue East Southwest, Winter Haven, FL 33880.

Southwest Florida Paddling Club, 20991 South Tamiami Trail, Estero, FL 33928.

Tampa Sea Kayakers, P.O. Box 12263, St. Petersburg, FL 33713–2263.

Florida Keys Paddling Club, 104050 Overseas Highway, Key Largo, FL 33037; (305) 451–3018.

Appendix E

Books Related to Florida and Paddling in Florida

Camping

Grow, G. *Florida Parks Guide to Camping Nature.* 6th edition (Longleaf Publications, 1997).

Molloy, J. *The Best Tent Camping in Florida* (Manasha Ridge Press, 1998).

Everglades

Fergus, Charles. *Swamp Screamer* (New York: North Point Press, 1996.) A well-written account of efforts to trace and monitor the endangered Florida panther in the Everglades of Southern Florida.

Matthiessen, Peter. *Killing Mister Watson* (New York: Vintage Books,

1991). A novel based on the real events surrounding the life of Mister Watson in the Everglades around the turn of the century.

Florida Keys

Ripple, Jeff. *The Florida Keys: The Natural Wonders of an Island Paradise* (Stillwater, MN: Voyageur Press, 1995). Excellent photographs and written descriptions of the natural history of the Florida Keys.

Williams, Joy. *The Florida Keys, A History and Guide.* 8th edition (Fodor's New York, 1997). An excellent general guide book about the Florida Keys.

Fossils

Brown, Robin C. *Florida's Fossils: Guide to Location, Identification & Enjoyment* (Sarasota FL: Pineapple Press, 1988). This is an excellent and easy to use book on local fossil identification. It provides good photographs.

History

Dickinson, Jonathan. *A True Story of Shipwreck and Torture on the Florida Coast in 1696* (Port Salerno: Florida Classics Library, 1985). Includes Jonathan Dickinson's original account of the events leading to and following the shipwreck that left his group and family stranded on the beach of southeast Florida and faced with hostile Indians.

Heisel, Tony, and Frank Oppel, eds. *Tales of Old Florida* (Secaucus, NJ: Castle, 1987). A fascinating collection of accounts and articles written around the turn of the century about hunting, fishing, wildlife, work, and travel in Florida.

Perry, I. Mac. *Indian Mounds You Can Visit* (St. Petersburg: Great Outdoors Publishing Company, 1993). This provides some basic information about some 165 aboriginal sites on the west coast of Florida.

Natural History

Bell, C. R. & B. J. Taylor. *Florida Wildflowers and Roadside Plants* (Chapel Hill: Laurel Hill Press, 1982).

Griggs, Jack. *All the Birds of North America* (New York: HarperCollins, 1997).

Moher, P. E. *Rare and Endangered Biota of Florida, Volume III. Amphibians and Reptiles* (Gainsville: University Press of Florida, 1992).

Nellis, David W. *Seashore Plants of South Florida and the Caribbean* (Sarasota, FL: Pineapple Press, 1994). By no means an exclusive flora, this book does detail ninety-four seashore plants, and includes some interesting information about many of the plants you will come across when paddling in Southern Florida.

Nelson, G. *The Shrubs and Woody Vines of Florida* (Sarasota, FL: Pineapple Press, 1996).

Nelson, G. *The Trees of Florida* (Sarasota, FL: Pineapple Press, 1994.

Penny, J. and J. G. Penny. *Sierra Club Guide to the Natural Areas of Florida* (San Francisco: Sierra Club Books, 1992).

Peterson, Roger Tory. *A Field Guide to the Birds (Eastern and Water Birds)* (Boston: Houghton Mifflin Company, 1934).

Paddling Manuals and Guides

Bannon, J. *Sea Kayaking Florida and the Georgia Sea Islands* (Asheville, NC: Out There Press, 1998).

Bergen, Brooksie and John. *Carefree Canoeing in Florida.* (Houston: Gulf Publishing, 1997). A guide to trails and outfitters.

Foster, Nigel. *Kayaking: A Beginners Guide.* 2nd ed. (Arundel: Fernhurst Books, 1999). A step-by-step guide to all the basic kayaking maneuvers. Descriptions are backed up by photographic sequences.

Foster, Nigel. *Nigel Foster's Sea Kayaking* (Old Saybrook, CT: The Globe Pequot Press, 1997). A thorough manual to the skills and background required for safe sea kayaking, with many illustrations and photographs.

Foster, Nigel. *Open Canoe Technique* (Arundel: Fernhurst Books, 1996). A comprehensive manual of open canoe skills, including paddling techniques, poling, rescues and open water safety.

Gluckman, D. *Sea Kayaking in Florida* (Sarasota, FL: Pineapple Press, 1995).

Index

About the Author

Nigel Foster has been kayaking and canoeing since he was a teenager. Considered one of the most charismatic and talented instructors in the world today, his lectures and classes attract large audiences of sea kayakers at all levels throughout the United States and Europe. The author of several kayaking and canoeing books and of many articles on paddling, he also designs kayaks and kayaking gear. Nigel's books include *Nigel Foster's Sea Kayaking* (Globe Pequot, 1997); and *Nigel Foster's Surf Kayaking* (Globe Pequot, 1998).

Through years of paddling in places as wild and far flung as Iceland, Arctic Norway, and Baffin Island, and in places as serene as Sweden and as pleasantly warm as Florida, Foster has developed an eye for identifying what is unique and special about individual paddling areas, and frequently writes about them for *Sea Kayaker* magazine. From his years of guiding groups in Wales, Scotland, and further afield, he has developed an uncanny appreciation for what paddlers of all experience levels will enjoy.